~ May yo[illegible]
joy in every
living.
Best Wishes!
Viki Vestuto

The Joy of Living an Organized Life

THE JOY OF LIVING AN ORGANIZED LIFE

A Guide to Help You Save Time and Money

Victoria Vestuto

SEABOARD PRESS
JAMES A. ROCK & COMPANY, PUBLISHERS

The Joy of Living an Organized Life: A Guide to Help You Save Time and Money
by Victoria Vestuto

SEABOARD PRESS

is an imprint of JAMES A. ROCK & CO., PUBLISHERS

Address comments and inquiries to:
SEABOARD PRESS
9710 Traville Gateway Drive, #305
Rockville, MD 20850

E-mail:
jrock@rockpublishing.com lrock@rockpublishing.com
Internet URL: www.rockpublishing.com

Trade Paperback ISBN: 978-1-59663-572-2

Library of Congress Control Number: 2007928322

Printed in the United States of America

First Edition: 2008

I would like to dedicate this book
to God
for giving me such a wonderful family
and for my analytical mind.
Together, they have allowed me to
document my experiences
in order to share them
with others

Table of Contents

CHAPTER 1

Set Your Course
The Fundamentals

Congratulations! By reading this book, you have made a decision to bring some joy into your life. And it won't take long for you to start experiencing that joy. Life throws each of us a lot of curve balls on top of the already routine tasks we must complete to live even a simple life. The idea behind this book is to put processes in place that will automate and streamline those routine tasks so we'll have more time, money and energy to handle the curve balls. By choosing to follow even a few ideas in this book, you will begin to reap the benefits. Let's get started!

There are some basic fundamentals of being organized that everyone has but there may be a better way to implement them. The fundamentals really need to work the same way you work. If you currently have a "To Do" list, please still read this chapter. You may pick up an idea or two that can either be added to your current "To Do" method, or it may be time to scratch it and start with a new way of thinking. This chapter covers some successful implementations of managing information and tasks by using "To Do" lists, and/or a spiral notebook (for your purse or briefcase or pocket) and/or a filing system. When you adopt any of the ideas listed in this chapter, you will immediately feel a sense of accomplishment.

When you have successfully implemented a great "To Do" system, you'll feel a weight lifted from your shoulders! You'll be able to accomplish more with less thinking time (confusion!) and what a joy that will bring to you!

The Dreaded "To Do" List

It's not enough to have a "To Do" list. Although it is a good start, the list can quickly become overwhelming if you place everything on it at one time. Then the list becomes less effective. There is a way to manage that list and become efficient at accomplishing the items on the list. The ideas in this chapter are implemented for visual people who like to use paper and pen, but there is no reason why you couldn't take the ideas and implement the system on your computer or PDA device using its "To Do" or "Tasks" function, or spreadsheet software. I encourage you to implement the entire "To Do" process and to customize it to meet your specific needs. Here are the steps.

1. The White Board

By placing all the items that go through your head in one location, you will feel a great sense of relief without becoming overwhelmed. The White Board is the one place to capture ALL your items, even if you don't plan on doing them for a while (I never want to lose one of my thoughts).

To begin, buy a white board and some dry-eraser markers in five or six different colors, including black. Using the black marker, divide your White Board into five columns. Label each column with a different color and title them:

- Someday
- Sooner than Later
- Social
- Quarterly
- Places to Go

Fill in each column with your entire "To Do's."

- In the "Someday" column, write down anything that comes to mind that you'd really like to do "Someday." This may include painting a room, mending a coat, checking into insurance policies, cleaning out the garage, organizing a closet, researching an item (i.e. appliance) etc. Make sure you get everything out of your mind and onto this column.
- Next, work on the "Sooner than Later" column. Write down the more immediate "To Do" items, i.e. making a dentist appointment, reading a book, calling for service on an item, buying something, a craft, decorating a room in your house, events, cleaning tasks, baking for an event etc. If appropriate, write down the month that item needs to be accomplished in front of the item. For example, a list item could be "pruning the evergreen bushes" and you need to do this in April before the new growth shows on the bushes.

- In the "Social" column, write down the people you'd like to get together with from a social perspective. You know you'd like to get together with a friend that you don't often get to see. Write their name down in this column.
- The "Quarterly" column can be used for things you want to do on a scheduled bases. There are some friends I like to write to (or email) that I don't want to forget to do so I place their names in this column. Quarterly items can also be house chores like cleaning out or organizing closets, or attacking a sewing pile.
- And finally, in the "Places to Go" column, write down local places you'd like to go or places you'd like to take your family. This may include a children's museum, the zoo, a water park or other ideas that you've heard from your friends. Also write down the hours of the location, phone number and directions if it's a new place to you.

Note that sometimes there are "supporting" documents which go with a "To Do" item. If you wish, you can go one step further and purchase paper stackers (plastic paper holders that stack on top of each other) or file folders. You'll need at least three. Use one for the "Someday" papers and another for the "Sooner than Later" papers. If you do this then you'll always know where to look when you're working on a "To Do" item. The third stacker or folder can be used to hold all your "reading materials" like magazines or newsletters that you get that you'd like to read but aren't time-critical. An additional usage can include keeping track of store or catalog coupons.

2. What I Can Accomplish List

Take a piece of paper and divide it into three columns. Title the columns "Calls," "Go," and "Do."

Take a *few* items from the "Sooner than Later" column on the White Board and arrange them in these categories:

- What phone calls do I need to make?
- What errands do I need to run?
- What tasks do I need to accomplish?

Review the other columns on the White Board (Someday, Social etc.) and, if appropriate, add one or two items. Now, erase these entries from the White Board.

Be sure to include the phone numbers for the items in the "Calls" column. Don't put the phone number on a *separate* piece of paper — you'll end up never making the phone call because you can't find the paper!

3. This Week's List

Now we tackle the "What to accomplish this week" question by making the "To Do" list.

Take another piece of paper and divide it into seven columns, one for each day of the week. Label each column with the day (M, T, W, etc.) and the date (10, 11, 12, etc.).

Now, take a look at your "What I Can Accomplish" list. Select an item and enter it in a column day. *Don't overwhelm yourself.* You don't have to place all items on this week's list—just the realistic ones. It may help to divide the days into "day" and "night."

Don't forget to add some time for *yourself.* Is there a book you want to read or a craft you want to work on? Block this time out on the weekly list. You'll find it useful to allot time for those "extra" things— otherwise, they won't get done. For example, if you *don't* schedule it, you may focus on your crafts and never get a chance to read a good book. You can even dedicate a regular time "block" for reading and another for crafts, and so on.

As the week progresses, update the "What I Can Accomplish" list by crossing off each entry when you complete the task. If you really get a sense of accomplishment by crossing items off a list, then cross it off "This Week's List" as well.

The Slash Folder

It's helpful to have a "Slash Folder" associated with "This Week's List." This folder will contain any relevant documents and/or information you'll need to accomplish the task on the list. Documents might include catalogue pages, receipts, phone numbers, emails, insurance claims, etc. You may have already stored these items in the paper stackers discussed in "The White Board" section.

> *Examples.* If you need to make a call regarding an insurance question, make sure you have your insurance statement in the slash folder. If you plan to order something from a catalog, have the page from the catalog with the item and the phone number in the Slash Folder.

The goal is to keep all relevant documents in *one place* so you can quickly complete the tasks on the "To Do" item. I take this one step further and carry the Slash Folder in a small tote bag or leave it in the car that I usually drive. I might even include a book that I 'm reading in the tote bag. You never know when you'll have a few spare minutes (while waiting for the kids) to accomplish a "To Do" or read a good book!

This Week's List for Children

You can also create a "This Week's List" for your children. Create a weekly schedule, display it in a prominent place and the children may look there instead of asking you what's going on. Using a schedule may help clarify everyone's expectations.

> *Examples:* Schedule Monday, Wednesday and Friday nights as shower nights. With luck, any complaints they have will dissipate since the expectation is made clear. Consider including items such as "No Video Games" on certain days or schedule tasks such as "Clean Out Garage." We even write down what days certain TV shows may be viewed. Include when a baby sitter is coming in this schedule. Be creative here — the more expectations you can document, the fewer questions you'll be fielding from your kids.

4. Repeat

Each week create a fresh "This Week's List" from the items on the "What I Can Accomplish" list. When that list is empty, or needs to be refreshed, go back to the White Board and create a new "What I Can Accomplish" list.

Don't feel bad if you must carry over items from the previous list. That's not a bad thing and you are still keeping track of the task. Feel free to re-categorize tasks when necessary. Go back to the White Board and rearrange tasks from "Sooner than Later" to the "Someday" column if you wish.

Be realistic and use the White Board as your "master" list for all "TO DO" tasks, both present and future.

5. In Progress

I have extended this "To Do" list method by one more level which I call "In Progress." This is optional but provides another avenue of fast retrieval.

If there's still room on your White Board, then add a column called "In Progress." Use this space to track tasks which cannot be completed until something occurs which is outside your immediate control. Use a separate piece of paper if you're out of room on the White Board.

I list items like Rebates or Returns (waiting for the credit), passports, programs I've signed up for but haven't received confirmation, and magazine subscriptions that I've cancelled. I also have a "slash" folder containing all the associated paperwork in case I need to refer to them.

That's it! If you follow these steps, you'll be surprised at how much you can accomplish and how easy it is.

A Work "To Do" List However You Define "Work"!

If you have a job or volunteer position where you interact with several people, an organized "To Do" list is important. You may capture these "To Do" items in an electronic spreadsheet. Create the columns with the following headings. *See Figure 1.*

Item #	Priority	What to Do	Who	Start Date	Due Date	Date Comp.	Comment
1	1	Have someone go through Vendor list and complete the form for each vendor.	JM	5/2	6/1		5/2: Sent JM an email with action item.
3	1	Verify the phone numbers for each vendor.	MG	5/6	5/10		5/6: Left VM with SSS asking for list.
4	2	Jane will give me the addresses for the vendors.	SV	5/6	5/12		
2	2	Schedule a meeting to review the vendor list.	JM	5/2	5/5	5/2	5/2: Meeting set for 5/12.

Figure 1: Create "To Do" items in an electronic spreadsheet.

Item #

Just a sequence number starting with the number 1. This column will eventually be "out of order" once you start accomplishing items and moving them off the list. But by having the sequence number, you are able to refer to this task from within other tasks.

Priority

Give yourself four task priorities:

1 = High

2 = Medium

3 = Low

4 = Complete

By assigning a "3" priority, you can capture tasks or ideas that you don't want to lose but they needn't be accomplished immediately.

What To Do

This column is usually large (wide) and describes the actual task at hand with as much detail as you need.

Who

Lists "who" is responsible for completing the task.

Start Date

The date you entered this item in the worksheet.

Due Date

The date on which the item must be accomplished.

Date Completed

The date that the item was actually completed.

Comments

Place any notes in this column, including the date of your comment. Include items such as a "spoke on the phone w/Joe," or "left a voicemail" or "a meeting is scheduled for …"

The key to this task sheet is to sort and track, electronically, the tasks via their priority number. Always arrange the "Priority 1" at the top of the list. In some cases, you'll have several different task lists, depending on how many projects you are managing.

Little Spiral Notebook

The disorganized person is typically *surrounded* by "piles" of documents and assorted pieces of paper. To avoid this, anytime you have a thought, write it down *and* organize it at the same time.

That's why the "Little Spiral Notebook" will become your main place for everything — every thought, errand, necessary purchase, etc. are stored in this little book.

> *Example:* I'm in a movie rental store, searching for a movie and becoming overwhelmed with all the choices. I remember that when I had lunch with my friend, she shared the name of a "must see" movie. Since my memory is bad, I wrote the name of the movie in my "Little Spiral Notebook" under the "Movies to see" page. I check the page and *voila* — I'm all set for an evening of *good* entertainment (instead of the "luck of the draw!" entertainment).

Once you have a little spiral notebook (5x3 inch), open it up and start dedicating pages to certain topics. The more "permanent" topics should go in back of the notebook while the more "volatile" topics go in front. As you "cross off" the things listed on your "volatile section" and have used up a page, simply rip out the page and dedicate the next available blank page to that same topic.

Some ideas for topics are listed below. Remember, the topics are to *remind* you of ideas that occur in everyday life and need a place to be filed. Think of each topic as a bucket in which the thoughts are grouped (organized) and stored.

> *Example:* Someone recommends a great restaurant. You can write the name of the restaurant under "To do with my husband (or friend)," or you might think of someone you'd like to get together with so you'd write the restaurant name under "Social list."

Does your mind ever wander while you're driving or riding the train or bus? Have your "Little Spiral Notebook" nearby to capture and organize your thoughts. Sometimes ideas and notes you capture in the "Little Spiral Notebook" should be transferred to the White Board where they can be processed as one of your "To Do" items.

- Errands to run. (v)
- Things to buy. (v)
- To Do's—general. (v)
- To Do with my husband or friend. (v)
- Social list—who would I (we) like to see soon. (v)
- Call—whom do I need to call soon. (v)

- Movies to see. (v)
- If on sale, buy … for things you need but not right away. (either v or p)
- If at a garage sale, look for … (v)
- Good prices and where, i.e. store x sells diapers at $3.99. (p)
- To Do's—around the home. (p)
- Some day when I have time … (p)
- Gift ideas for yourself/family. List the person's initials and then the item. (p)
- Gift ideas for others. List the person's name then the item. (p)
- Clothing sizes for family (especially useful around the holidays and birthdays). (p)
- Authors or books you like or have been recommended. (p)
- Kids birthday "lists" or ideas. (v)
- Questions to ask your doctor/pediatrician. (v)
- Wines I like and where to buy them. (p)

Any time you have a "random" thought, capture it here in the Random Thoughts (v) category. These are notions that cross your mind when you're driving or daydreaming and don't fit in any other category. If you have a coupon you plan to use soon, store it in the little notebook where it will be readily available the next time you're at the store. Use the "Little Spiral Notebook" as a tool to omit the need for little pieces of paper (where you've written important thoughts but lost the paper before you could use it).

File Drawer

Even if you already have a filing drawer, read this section. A simple but great tool to any organizer is the filing cabinet or drawer. But, the key to its success is the topic or arrangement of the each file. The more specific and appropriate the file name, the better the file drawer system works.

A filing system is important for two reasons: quick storage and quick retrieval.

> *Example:* As you read through magazines or newspapers, clip articles about travel spots that interest you and file these in your file drawer instead of piling them up where you'll never look at them again! You'll be surprised at the "Places to Visit" folder and how many entries are in it, if you adopt this system.

You don't have to run out and buy a filing cabinet — a cardboard box will do as long as it can hold hanging folders. If you accumulate lots of files (which really is a good thing), then simply pull those files which you use most frequently and keep them in a table-top file holder. The idea is to provide easy access (for filing and retrieval) since you use these files frequently.

Below are some suggested categories for file topics.

- *Address/Phone numbers.* For all those names/places/numbers you don't keep in your address book or cell phone but are nice to have, i.e. catalog phone numbers, 1-800 numbers, charities.

- *Children.* This can be broken down into sections such as pregnancy, 0-12 months, 1-5 years, Elementary school age, JR. High age, Teenagers. Any articles or information you get for these age groups can be stored here.
- *Children, Information.* Keep one folder for each child. Use this to store medical information, SSN, school records, etc.
- *Cleaning tips.* Articles you have taken out of magazines, family "secret formulas" for how to clean XYZ.
- *Day Care.* Use to store the handbook and any contract information or receipts.
- *Decorating.* This can be broken down into further topics, such as painting, wallpapering, and furniture. You can store pictures of furniture you like or wallpaper examples in these folders.
- *Directions.* Any time you print out or write down directions, save them! Try to be good about writing down the place name and phone number on the piece of paper.
- *Financial.* This can also be broken down into several sections and can contain your bank statements, investment statements, etc.
- *Forms.* Keep items like insurance claims, UPS or USPS slips or other forms you have to fill out on a periodic basis.
- *Games/Jokes.* Save them in this folder, especially if you have a bad memory!

- *Gardening.* If you like gardening there is a lot of information out there on this topic. Even if you have a small backyard garden, you'll find newspaper articles about bugs or treatments that could be helpful to have on hand.
- *Home Improvement.* Keep the receipts or bills from any home improvement or repair in your house. This can later be used when you go to sell your house. Take it one step further … Keep a separate piece of paper in this file where you document the item. This sheet becomes the summary page and the items you file are the supporting documents.
- *Home Purchases.* Purchases while living in a house (i.e. furniture receipts). This is different from the home improvement file. This file is just for major items in the house that are not tax related but you want to keep the receipt.
- *Home Repair Articles.* Anything you clip from magazines or journals, store here.
- *Landscaping.* If you see something you like from a magazine or newspaper, keep it here. Or, if you ever have a landscaper to your house, keep their literature — they usually provide you with a great brochure on all types of bushes and trees. Also include in this folder any proposals you have had from landscaping firms and any thoughts that you've had about them. For instance, I had two proposals and neither com-

pany ever followed up with them so I made a note of that (I wanted a "pro-active" landscaping company).

- *Landscaping-Mulch.* Include notes such as where you have recently purchased mulch in yards (i.e. a truck load of mulch). If you do some research, you'll notice a variation of prices of mulch and their associated delivery charges. Make notes of these and highlight which ones you have done business with and if you like them etc.

  If you have ever ordered mulch by the yard, also include in this folder a diagram of your house and its landscape. Make a note of how much mulch you purchased and what areas it covered. One summer, we bought mulch both by the truck load (yards) and by the bag. I made a note of what I was able to cover from the truck load (I used one color of a highlighter) and what was covered by the bags (another color highlighter). Now the next time I need to "do mulch" I have a clear understanding of how much I need.
- *Maps.* When you go out of town, keep the local rental car map and file it here. The detailed map may help you later when you visit that city again (i.e. looking up a street address or hotel location).
- *Medical Information.* Anytime you or a family member is sick, write it down! In this folder, place a piece of paper for each family member. It only has two columns. The first column will contain the words "Start" then the next row will

have "End." When someone gets sick, write down the start date and in the second column, a description of the illness. When that member is better, make sure you enter an end date. I cannot tell you how valuable this is for any physician to see a trend. It helped us tremendously when one of my children had constant nose bleeds (always in the middle of the night) and we could track its frequency.

- *Menus.* Gathered from local restaurants. Keep coupons for those restaurants in here.
- *Paint Samples.* Every time you paint a room, write down the manufacturer and color of the paint. Also store the "paint chip sample" if you have one. Put the name of the room on each paint chip sample. And as an aside, *always label* your paint cans (kitchen, outside back door, kids' bathroom).
- *Patterns.* If you sew or knit etc, store them all in one location.
- *Pets.* Keep any articles on any pets or information on your specific pet.
- *Product information.* Keep track of anything you may purchase in the future.
- *Product and warranty information.* This is GREAT. Use multiple folders (or an alphabetical "accordion" file) and place a couple of alphabetic dividers in each. As you receive a gift, toy, electronic gizmo, file the instructions and warranty under the correct letter (i.e. T for toaster). The

next time something breaks, you'll know where to find the repair number!

- *School.* Any communications from the children's school(s) are placed in here. Teacher's phone numbers and/or the school calendar can be filed here. Items such as sports schedules, including sports you're children aren't in, because you may wish to attend a game, may be filed here.
- *Special interests.* Hobbies (photography, crafts, knitting etc). Have one folder for each of your special interests.
- *Sports.* Hours of arenas, time schedules, phone numbers.
- *Stocks.* If you play the stock market at all, this folder will save you hours at tax time once you decided to sell your stocks. Every time you buy a stock, make sure you put the paper work immediately into this folder. When it comes time to sell, the IRS wants to know simple things like when you bought the stock, and at what price. This information isn't always on the paperwork when you go to sell. Place all related papers of the buy and sell of stocks in this folder.
- *Things I'd like to buy some day.* Have you ever seen something in a magazine that would be "nice to have"? Don't lose the idea! Take the picture and file it in this folder. One day you can compare all the "Things I'd like to buy some day" and discover that some aren't so important any more.

- *Things to do.* This covers places to go and/or "some day I'd like to do this." As you read articles in magazines or newspapers, clip them and file them here.
- *Vacation ideas.* If you see a good article, clip it and store!
- *Village/City News.* Parks and Recreation District brochures, Department information, phone numbers, etc.
- *Wedding Registries.* For friends and family; these are always handy for next year's holiday shopping list!

CHAPTER 2

In the Kitchen

Think how much time you spend in your kitchen. In some ways, I spend too much time in the kitchen and in other ways, I don't spend enough. What I mean is, while it does take a lot of *thought* to prepare three meals a day, 365 days a year, it doesn't *have* to. If you choose a few of the ideas listed in this chapter, you'll prepare those meals with less "thought" time and more "enjoy" time.

I used to find myself staring at a cookbook, simply not knowing *what* to make. Meal planning became an exercise in frustration. But here's the good news … it doesn't have to be that way!

This chapter is divided into the following sections: Planning, Shopping and Preparing a meal. If you can use at least one idea from each section, you will be pleasantly surprised at what happens … joy!

Planning: What to Eat

The best place to start is, of course, in the beginning! Do you ever find yourself making chicken three days a week because that's what you know you have in your freezer? I used to do that and realized my family was getting tired of chicken! (Frankly, so was I.)

So, to keep myself out of trouble and simplify meal-planning, I dedicate one day of the week to a different type of meal. For instance, Tuesday night is ground beef (hamburger) night, so I find a recipe that uses ground beef. This could be anything from tacos to meatloaf.

Sample Meal Planning:

Sunday	A new recipe or some special meal
Monday	Soup
Tuesday	Ground beef
Wednesday	Pasta
Thursday	Salad
Friday	Easy meal (ready-made or eat out!)
Saturday	Poultry

You can easily substitute the type of meal with what you eat most often (i.e. seafood) or use a 10-day rotation instead of a 7-day routine. It's also a good idea to keep a list of the frozen meats you currently have on-hand posted on your refrigerator door.

Recipes

So now that you know what types of meals you're going to prepare, you need to *organize* your recipes. There are plenty of good recipes out there — the trick is to have them easily accessible and knowing which ones are the really good ones. You can find interesting recipes in cookbooks, magazines, newspapers, and from friends. The internet is another excellent source of great cooking ideas.

What's Inside those Cookbooks?

Cookbooks are great, but can be very overwhelming. I have many cookbooks and some I had never opened. I didn't want to discard them (they might have something good inside), so I came up with a system.

Select a cookbook. Now take a large index card or sheet of lined paper and create some categories that coordinate with your meal-planning schedule. For example, include salads, soups, pasta, ground beef, poultry and "other." Tailor these categories to the type of cookbook you're using and, if you wish, add or substitute items such as vegetables, side dishes, breads and desserts. If you're using a "Pasta" cookbook, then you can still list regular categories such as pasta, salads, poultry, and ground beef.

Tape the index card or page to the inside cover of the cookbook. Later, when you have some free time, browse through the cookbook. When you see a recipe that looks interesting, write the *page number* on the card under the appropriate category.

Later, when you're planning meals, use this card or paper to try recipes from the cookbook. After you've completed a new recipe, be sure to *update* your reference card. If you didn't like it, cross the page number off of the index card. If it was a success, then underline the page number on the index card (to show that you prepared it) and *rate* the recipe.

Rating Meals

I use ratings 8–10 (I don't know why I started at 8). If it's an 8, then I'd make the recipe again but it wasn't great. I reserve 9 and 10 for the great ratings. You can also develop an expanded system for rating recipes. For example, you might highlight the page number if it's a good recipe for entertaining. (This can mean either ease of preparation and/or a great-tasting dish.) You might use a different highlight color if someone in your family especially liked it. This helps me with my children, knowing what recipes they will eat without complaining!

You may also develop codes for "difficulty," and "odd ingredients not usually on-hand" if you wish. I take the index card one step further by placing an "H" next to the recipe if it's good to bring to a friend in need (Hospitality). I also add a card to my index box that I describe in "A Shopping List Trick" section found later in this chapter.

This is a quick and easy way to tackle all those unused cookbooks. You'll find yourself actually "trying" new recipes and getting to know which cookbooks are most reliable. You may also be able to "weed" out some of those cookbooks you realize you don't need. If you have a run of bad luck with a cookbook, then copy the few recipes you liked (if any) and discard the cookbook or trade it in at a used book store for a new one. Removing the duds from your cookbook collection will allow you to use the best cookbooks and reduce clutter in the kitchen (some cookbooks can take up a lot of space).

Internet, Magazine or Newspaper Recipes

I enjoy browsing and looking for new recipes in magazines and newspapers. I've also discovered, on the the web, hundreds and hundreds of sites where I can find and print recipes. With a "system" now in place, I actually *try* the recipe instead of losing it or tossing it in a "I'll-go-through-that" pile someday.

To organize all those loose sheets of paper and clippings, take an "accordion" (expandable) file folder that has multiple pockets. Title the pockets: General Tips, Beverages, Meals, Poultry, Pork/Lamb, Hamburger, Sea Food, Salads/Pastas, Vegetables, Breads/Biscuits/Rolls and Desserts. As you read the magazine or newspaper, rip out the recipe you like, circle the title (in case there are several on one page but you're only interested in one), and file it in the recipe folder under the appropriate category. It's quick and easy, and simple to retrieve the recipe. Rate the recipe (give it a number rating) once you've tried it and don't forget to highlight the title if you think it's good for entertaining or if you receive any compliments on it.

It also helps to use a colored piece of paper or a file folder as a divider in each pocket category to separate recipes you've tried from those "yet unmade." I'm trying to go through all my recipes and by having that piece of paper as the divider, I just look through the recipes in front of the colored paper (yet unmade). Don't forget to throw the recipe away if it's no good. That way, your recipe file becomes more reliable.

Grocery Shopping

What a chore! And how often we go! This is a two-step process: the preparation/making of the shopping list and the actual act of shopping. If you do this correctly, however, it won't be overwhelming and you'll have a chance to save money. Just a few minutes of time can save you dollars with each trip to the grocery store.

Preparing the List

You know what types of meals you want to make using the Meal Planning Guide. You can just pick out your recipes and create the shopping list. That works. It is also a simple idea to always have a running shopping list on your refrigerator door (or somewhere handy). Any time you run out of something, immediately write it on the list. There is yet an additional approach you can use to create a shopping list very quickly.

A Shopping List Trick

Although I like to cook when I have time, I never really have time. Often, I skip new recipes because I'm missing some of the ingredients required. But, I don't want my family to "suffer" either, eating the same meals week after week.

So, I've come up with a compromise. Find a container (index box) that holds 3x5 index cards. Use index card dividers and title them: Poultry, Ground Beef, Pork, Lamb, Vegetables, Sea Food, Sirloin, Roasts, Pastas, Soup, and Others. Now, pick a few of your favorite recipes. Write the *name* of the recipe on the top left-hand side of the index card. On the right-hand side, write down the *source* for the recipe.

If the source is a cookbook, then write the book title and page number. If the recipe is from your accordion file folder, then write the words "Recipe File" and the category from which you took it (poultry, vegetables, etc.). Use the rest of the index card to note any ingredients that you'd typically not have on-hand in your kitchen (special spices, canned goods, etc.). Also include the type of meat (if any) and quantity (i.e. whole frying chicken).

When completed, file the index card under the appropriate category. The next time you go shopping, choose a few of the index cards and take them with you. You've just planned your menu and created your shopping list with very little work! Remember that you can use these cards repeatedly, saving even more time.

To ensure variety in meal-planning, once you've made that particular dish, move the index card to the *back* of the category. Then select index cards from the front of the category.

Feel free to add additional information to these cards to help you organize! For example, place an "H" or "E" next to the title on the index card if this recipe is good to bring to a friend (Hospitality) or if it's a great recipe to use for Entertainment. This way cooking for a friend in need (sick or just had a baby) or entertaining and choosing a menu, can by made just a little bit easier. Consider other information such as "Kid Friendly" or "Mom's Favorite."

So now, your shopping list has gotten even easier. You know what meals to plan by what day of the week it is. You just pull a recipe from the appropriate category in the container that you created in *A Shopping List Trick* section and off you go to the grocery store.

Coupons, Coupons, Coupons ...

If you already clip coupons and have a place to store them, ask yourself this question—how easy is it to bring the right coupons on your shopping trip? I have two versions of this system. One is a "skinny down" version and the other is a bit more involved. One of the two should fit your life style and budget but you'll save more money using the second approach.

The Simple Approach

The simple approach is to clip only frequently-used product coupons and place them in a letter-sized envelope. Keep this envelope in your car. You'll only be storing about 20 coupons at a time, so the size of the envelope shouldn't be an issue. If you find that you clip and save more coupons, then keep reading for another way to organize.

Another Way

If you're clipping and saving many coupons then perhaps you need to create a "Coupon Box." This isn't a new idea, but the Coupon Box is only effective if you can *easily and quickly* locate and retrieve the coupon so you can use it. This not only refers to ease of access, but also the logic of which *category* you file the coupon. If you're a coupon clipper, then you probably have some sort of carrier for your coupons. I like a large (4x6) version of an index box and cards because it allows for easy access.

Sub-Dividers

Try organizing your Coupon Box with Alphabetical Dividers. Then add Sub-Dividers within the Alphabetical Dividers. A Sub-Divider is another index card with a name of a frequently-used grocery item or group of items. For example. *Cat Food* and *Cat Litter* can be a Sub-Divider. When you're in the pet section at the store, both items are in the same area. By combining two related topics on a Sub-Divider, you don't have to jump around in your coupon box to find each item. Sub-Divider categories should also include items that you buy at the local drug store (personal sundries). Refer to

Appendix A for a list of recommended grocery Sub-Divider categories. After you have created your Sub-Dividers, file the coupon behind this category card.

To create a file space for anomalies (coupons with no sub-divider), make sure there is a *blank* index card at the end of every letter. When you clip a coupon for a less frequently-used item (with no corresponding category), you can store it behind the blank index card (just before the next alphabetic letter). For example, you buy biscuits only occasionally but you clipped a coupon for this item. File it at the end of the 'B' section in the Coupon Box behind the blank card.

Use a Pencil

Keep a pencil in your Coupon Box (also useful for checking things off of your grocery list). As you pull out the coupons for a given category, place your pencil in the coupon box as a placeholder. That just makes it easier to return the coupons to their proper location.

Expired Coupons

When you file your coupons, always place the newest coupon in the *back* of the section. Later, when you're shopping and searching for a particular coupon, throw out any expired coupons at the same time (I crumble them up and place in my pocket). If you do this consistently, all the "ready to expire" coupons will be in the front to be used first.

If you can follow this routine, then you'll get more out of your coupons and save money each time you shop. On average, I save $10–$20 per grocery trip shopping for only two people. That's worth the extra few minutes it takes to use coupons. Also, if you notice a coupon is about to expire and it's an item you use regularly, then go ahead and purchase it, even if it's not on your shopping list. Sometimes I've gone shopping and noticed that I'm just a day late from using several coupons and I was just in the grocery store last week.

Food Bargains

If you shop in multiple stores in order to save money, here's an easy trick to help you determine if that "sale price" is a good deal. Tape an index card on top of your coupon box (or use your PDA). Write the item that you'd like to purchase and next to it, the *sale* price that you've just seen in the store. For example, Store #1 has boneless skinless chicken breasts at $.99/lb. Store #2 has them for $1.29/lb. Later, when you're shopping and see boneless skinless chicken breasts on sale for $1.39, you'll know this isn't a great price.

Don't Buy What You Can't Cook

I was "guilty" of buying meats that were on sale. This doesn't sound bad, right? Well, I don't know much about the different cuts of meat and half the time, I'd buy some meat that I wasn't sure how to cook and couldn't readily find a recipe for it. Consequently, my "sale purchase" wasn't much of a bargain.

On the other hand, many recipes I used regularly called for expensive cuts of meat and I'd only buy those cuts when they were on sale. But now, I've wised up a bit.

I selected roughly 15 preferred recipes (ones I'd like to make anytime) but which required special cuts of meat (special here means "not ground beef!"). Then I took an index card (you can also use your PDA) and listed the different cuts of meat and quantity required for each recipe. If several recipes used the meat, then I just listed the quantities next to the meat type.

Now, when I'm grocery shopping and see a particular cut of meat on sale, I pull out my index card and see if I have a matching recipe.

Here are some examples:

Baby Back Pork Ribs (3 lbs)
Beef Eye of Round Roast (3 lbs)
Beef Tenderloin Steaks (4-4oz, 1 inch thick), (2-6 oz)
Boneless Rib Roast or Tenderloin (2¼ lbs)
Fillet of Beef (6 oz., 1½ inch thick)
Flank Steak (1 lb), (1½ lbs), (3/4 lb)

In the example above, Flank Steak has three recipes associated with it.

As a final thought, instead of using an index card, you might want to add this to a page in your "Little Spiral Notebook" from Chapter 1.

A Simple Grocery Shopping Tip

The next time you go grocery shopping, have your groceries bagged as follows: cold items in plastic and the rest in paper bags. This way, when you get home, you'll know what to unpack first (before you get interrupted) and you won't have to go running back and forth between cabinets, pantry and refrigerator. Just park yourself in front of the fridge with all the plastic bags and start unpacking.

Short Cuts and Time Savers

When you chop one onion, chop a few more. Measure in either ¼ cup or ½ cup increments and place in a freezer bag. This way you are only cleaning and cutting once for multiple recipes.

Ground Beef

Buy ground beef in bulk. Then divide by weight and store/freeze in varying increments, from ¼ lb. to 1 lb. For the smaller, ¼ lb. portions, make hamburger patties, wrap in wax paper and plastic wrap individually. This way, you'll always have hamburger patties available for dinner or, when a recipe calls for ¾ lb of ground beef, you can easily pull out three patties.

For larger quantities, wrap and make sure you mark them, including the date of purchase.

Miscellaneous

Depending on the type of cooking you do, you may find it helpful to take a can of tomato paste and separate it into one-tablespoon portions. Place each portion on wax paper, freeze, and then wrap, individually, in a baggie or foil, for future use. This way you won't have to waste a whole can of tomato paste the next time you need a tablespoon for a recipe.

Keep a list of frozen meats on your refrigerator door along with the date of purchase. This way you won't have to guess what's inside your freezer or how long you've had it.

Another Time-Saving Tip

Sometimes, when you have a lot of leftovers, it's actually nice to give some of them to your guests. The same holds true for dishes you prepare for friends. It can be a mixed blessing, however, if the recipients feel that they must wash and return the dishes to you.

A couple of suggestions might work to help solve this dilemma. The next time you're out garage sale shopping, go ahead and buy those extra plates or bowls. Usually you can pick these up for 50 cents or less. Use these and tell the recipients that they can keep the dishes!

Also, you can wash and store the tinfoil pie pans from the frozen pie shells or plastic containers (from cold salads, deli salads, sour cream, etc.). Using the plastic containers or pie tins is not as glamorous as the garage sale dishes, but your friends won't feel guilty about recycling them or throwing them away!

CHAPTER 3

Great Uses for Index Cards

These handy-dandy cards are great for getting organized. Keep in mind, however, that as you read an idea, you can decide if it's better for you to use an electronic device (computer, PDA) to store the information. It all depends on how much you like to type versus writing information by hand. Also, always store the information so that it is handy! The concept is essentially the same, whether you use index cards or store the same information electronically. Here are a few ways you can become more organized.

Baby Announcements

When you receive a baby announcement, write the parents' name as the title on an index card. Then, add the baby's name and birth date (and any other pertinent information) on the card. The next time those parents have a baby, add it to the index card. This gives you a quick reference of how many kids and their ages. You can store the index cards in a standard-size envelope. I keep the envelope on my desk or near the address book.

Contributions

My family has about ten charities to which we donate money. We like to donate to each of them, equally. I was a little frustrated when I couldn't keep track of which charity I'd most recently made a donation. Thus, I started to "tip the scale" from one charity to another. To solve that problem, I took a lined index card and listed a brief name of the charity on the left hand side, one per row. Each time I make a contribution to a charity, I put a check mark next to its name. The card provides a running tally of how often I have donated to the charity. If you wish, you could expand the idea and write the dollar amount given instead of the simple check mark. You could also could write the date of the donation as well. If you note both of these items, it might help you when it comes to tax time. Create a new card for each calendar year.

For more ideas, see Chapter 4, "Donations, Cash or Credit" section.

Directions

This applies to information which you don't receive via electronic means (those that would be stored in a file folder as described in Chapter 1).

Any time you receive directions from an individual, write them down on an index card. Take the card with you when you travel to verify the instructions. Update, correct or clarify the information. if necessary. Then store the card someplace that is readily accessible the next time you're traveling to that location.

Keep all your addresses *together*. That way, when you visit Aunt Alma's house once a year for the holidays, you won't show up late because you were lost! These cards are particularly useful for places you visit *infrequently*. Use these index card directions for in- as well as out-of-state destinations.

Internet Shopping

If you shop on the internet, especially for clothes, create an index card for each site from which you place orders. For each clothing site, write on the card "pants," "shirts," "skirts," "shoes" and any other item that you may purchase from this site. As you buy items, write down the *size* on the card. For example, at Land's End, you may wear a size 10 in their jeans but, when shopping at the Gap, you may need a size 8 instead. This is true for each individual item. Remember that a "large" size is not the same "large" size at all the stores. You will find that you're returning items less frequently (and who enjoys returning items from the internet!). Don't forget to specify on the card which family member the item/size applies to.

You can also add notes to these cards if you find seasonal sales. I know some sites offer free shipping at certain times of the year and one site even offered 50% off everything online! Why pay full-price when you don't have to!

Consider creating a special email address which you use strictly for shopping on the internet. This may prevent some SPAM from heading your way. Use one of the internet sites that offer free email accounts. You can always forward your mail (shopping confirmations, shipping information) to your "real" email address. For more information, see Chapter 4, "Internet Credit Card" section.

Major Holidays & Events

My memory is bad, especially concerning annual events. But I do want to remember good bargains or tricks that I've learned! So I have created index cards for different seasons and times of the year which is use to keep track of important information.

Although there are a ton of sales after Christmas, some are significantly better than others (this is true for any holiday, really). When I discovered a post-Christmas sale on wrapping paper for 25¢ or 50¢ at a certain store, I made a note on my Christmas index card so that I can check this store first, before I look for further bargains. You can also use the card to record the number of Christmas cards you need (I ordered too few this year and now know better for next year ... but will I remember? Now I will.). Jot down your best cookie recipe or oddball things like "what is a good time to start the holiday party?" Use the card to note where you bought your Christmas tree and include whether you'd go there again or where you can buy a live garland. These cards are a handy place to keep track of information for those once-a-year events.

These index cards are also handy for other occasions including (but not limited to): Valentine's Day, Easter, Mother's Day, Father's Day, 4th of July, and Thanksgiving.

On my 4th of July card, I have listed the places that have fireworks and the dates (in the past, one village has fireworks on the 3rd of July), where to park, what time to go, and even where to sit! The vacation card is handy if you think you will return to the same place in the future. You can write notes about what you want to see on the next trip or lessons learned from the first one. On one of our trips, we learned about a great bakery and craft store. We were not able to visit them but we'd like to stop in the next time we're in the area.

Other Events

I have an "Apple Picking Card" where I've listed the different places we've visited, directions, driving time, as well as whether we liked them and what extra activities (if any) they offered. I've even documented how many apples to pick! We ended up with two bushels and, for us, that was too many (I ended up throwing away some apples). Next year, I'll know we only need 1½ bushels. The same idea can be applied to a Pumpkin Farm.

Funeral Card

A funeral card is very handy. Here are some suggested notes you can write on that card:

- Make a meal for the bereaved family
- Make some cookies for the bereaved family
- Send a card
- Send flowers to a family member
- Make a "Meal Basket"

A Meal Basket is a great treat. During the bereavement period, food is often not a high priority, yet it is a necessity. A Meal Basket contains ingredients for a family meal. For example: small bag of carrots, small bag of celery, an apple, an orange, a few bananas, sausage, sliced cheese, lettuce, pepper, avocado, kiwi, garlic bulb, bread sticks, Italian bread, salad dressing, spaghetti, spaghetti sauce, cheese crackers, coffee, risotto, wine, parmesan cheese, crackers, dried fruit, croutons, fruit juice, olives and some candy.

Month Cards

You may also add index cards which are arranged by month. For example, the April index card would include "bush trimming" or specific yard work. I discovered that we have an apple tree in our yard and I just learned that they must be pruned in February. I use my "February" card to remind me of this task. Here are some examples:

February	Prune apple tree
April	Prune evergreens, except pines
	Best price for annuals at: ABC store $2.99 a flat
August	Backpacks are on sale at XYZ store
	Football practice started on MM/DD/YY last year
October	Where to buy pumpkins
	Water evergreens until the first frost
	When leaves have fallen, prune trees

Special Washing Instructions

I have ruined too many clothes to not pass this tidbit along. When you buy clothes that have special washing instructions, make a note of the garment item on an index card and include the special instructions. Create a "Master List" in order to keep track of your index cards. Take a piece of paper and write down a detailed description of the garment. You may choose to organize the master list by family member, e.g. "Mom has a washable green silk blouse" or "Dad has a 100% cotton Polo shirt." Post the Master List in plain view by the washing machine and store the index cards nearby where they are easily accessible.

For quick recognition, you can use permanent markers and make a color dot on the label of each washing items. For example, if there is a washing card associated with that item, use a color dot. It that item needs cold water only or the gentle cycle, use another color marker or a different shape (star). By marking the items ahead of time, washing them *correctly* will become a little easier.

Suitcase/Packing and More

Although I don't travel a lot, my family and I do travel some. I never seem to leave enough time for packing and I'm always afraid I am going to forget something! There are actually two parts to packing. The first part is *what to pack*, and the second part is *how to pack*.

What to Pack

There are two ways you can attack the *what to pack* part. The first little trick is to start a 4x6 index card for each member of your family (or type a list on the computer and print it out). On the card, write down the items that you'll need to pack. Remember that the more details you include, the less thinking you have to do later. Refer to the "What to Wear" section, later in this Chapter, to assist you in deciding what clothes/outfits to pack.

An example is listed below. Leave some space after each item for a check mark. As you pack, use a pencil and check off those items already in the suitcase. I usually pack some things ahead of time, but others must wait until the day of the trip (when everything is time-critical). Check the card on the day of your departure and it will help you remember those last-minute items. Don't forget to *update* the cards as you go, should you find that you left an item off of the list.

Mom: Jewelry, outfit1, outfit2, outfit3, outfit4, outfit5, slips, nylons, socks, under garments, shoes, money, contact cleaning solution, makeup (you can go into more detail here), deodorant, pajamas, hairbrush, toothbrush, toothpaste, soap, shampoo, razor, tweezers, bathing suit, bathing suit cover-up, day timer, nail polish and remover and cotton balls, medicine, purse, reading materials

Dad: outfit1, outfit2, outfit3, outfit4, outfit5, socks, under garments, shoes, money, contact cleaning solution, Doppler bag, deodorant, after shave, pajamas, hairbrush, toothbrush, toothpaste, soap, shampoo, razor, bathing suit, day timer, medicine, reading materials

Baby: outfit1, outfit2, outfit3, outfit4, outfit5, extra clothes, pajamas, shoes, diapers, socks, slippers, swimsuit, diapers, diaper cream, bottles, nipples, pacifier, formula, baby food, bibs, crackers (food), juices, medicine (aspirin), stroller, car seat, blankets, pajamas, toys, books, toothbrush, shampoo, baby lotion, baby oil, bath toys, plastic plates, baby silverware, sand toys

Kids: books, puzzles, toys, stuffed animals, videos/ DVDs

All: Sunglasses, hats, coats, vitamins, water shoes

Miscellaneous: address book, atlas or map, backpack, camera(s), car phone, food, laundry detergent, money, pens and pencils, rafts or pool stuff, sunscreen, waist bag, water bottle, hotel information, walkie talkies (2-way radios)

The second trick to attack *what to pack* requires a computer. Open a spreadsheet for "Packing." Create three columns with the titles "What," "Who" and "Packed?" In the "What" column, list the item (pajamas, underwear, etc.). In the "Who" column, use an initial (or brief abbreviation) to identify the family member or, in some cases, "All" if everyone in the family needs the item. (The term "All" is most useful when you intend to pack for everyone in one pass.) Use the "Packed?" column for making a checkmark, once the item has been packed. If this is an "All" row (i.e., pajamas or socks), then use initials to indicate for whom the item has been packed. When you are ready to begin packing in earnest, it's helpful to sort the spreadsheet by "Who" in order to gather all items at once for each family member.

Walkie Talkies and Backpacks

I cannot stress enough how important a backpack and walkie talkies can be to making a vacation successful, especially if you have small children. If you are planning any sort of outings on your trip (zoo, amusement park, etc.) having a backpack can save the day. You can pack water bottles, change of clothes, snacks and maps in the backpack. The walkie talkies are great if you have more than one child and may have to separate from them at any part of the day. We had several cases where dad would take one child to one part of the park (age appropriate) and I'd take the other in a different direction. The walkie talkies just made that separation so much simpler.

Warm Weather Destination

Here is another little "tid-bit" of experience. If you happen to be traveling to a warm place, select "light" colored tops or shirts. I made a bad decision when I packed navy blue T-shirts for my boys. The sun just baked them when we spent the entire day at an amusement park. Gray T-shirts would have been a much better choice (and they don't get as dirty as white ones).

Lesson Learned

And a word of advice—do pack a little bit of powdered laundry detergent. Some hotels may have some sort of laundry facility (or there is always a Laundromat). I try to pack lightly and gamble that my kids aren't going to spill ketchup on their shorts. But when they do, and when I have run out of clean shorts, I can be prepared and use a washer and dryer. The laundry facility probably sells detergent, but it might not be your brand of preference (or allergies) and it's going to cost 100% more than it should.

Packing Food

If you travel to a place where you bring your own groceries or do your own cooking, it helps to include food items on your Packing List. This will be your "grocery list" for what to buy when you arrive at your destination, or your packing list if you're taking your groceries from home. You may want to take some basic staples such as salt, pepper, sugar, etc. Also, by having this list, it becomes your meal planner for the vacation. You've already thought about what you are going to prepare for the week (simple meals!) by making a grocery list in advance.

You can print a new spreadsheet for each trip that you take and update it with new items when necessary.

How to Pack

This is just as important as *what to pack*. If you are traveling by air and plan to check more than one suitcase, you should prepare for the worst ... a lost piece of luggage. The best way to anticipate this calamity is to sort clothes, as you pack, by outfit and person. Pack each suitcase so that you distribute your outfits evenly. For example, set out shorts, t-shirts, underwear, and socks for each member of the family. Pack this in the first suitcase and repeat for the next round. Each suitcase should have several changes of clothes for everyone. You'll have to make some decisions about where to pack pajamas, etc. Pack critical items such as medicines, tooth brushes, etc., in a small carry-on for the plane.

Another trick is to pack what you need for the day that you arrive in one suitcase. For example, we traveled to San Diego and arrived early at the hotel, around noon. We were unable to check-in for several hours. Fortunately, I'd packed our swimsuits, water shoes, shorts and so forth, in the purple suitcase so we were able to change and head for the beach to enjoy the rest of the day.

Return Trip

To make things just a bit easier on your return trip, try to pack all the dirty clothes in one suitcase and any clean clothes in another. That way, one suitcase goes straight to the laundry room while the other can be unpacked first.

Technology Trick

With the way technology has become so sophisticated and with all the power packed into a small device, I simply cannot remember how to use all the features of "the new technology." The digital camera, for instance—there are many options on that "thing" which I use infrequently. But I did buy *that* camera because of its features.

In order to get a handle on these features, I read the digital camera's User Guide and make short notes on a 3x5 index card. I use the front side to document the features I'll use more often and the back side for the less-frequent but still important functions. I keep the index card in the camera bag. I also have an index card for my digital video camera and I'm thinking about adding one for my cell phone. You can create a card for your DVD or VCR recording devices as well as any other hi-tech items.

Wedding Trick

Great organizational skills are needed in preparing for a wedding. One trick to get you through this hectic time is to write the name of every guest you are planning to invite on an index card. For each card, indicate:

- When you sent the invitation
- When you received a response to the invitation (include particulars, i.e., how many guests, etc.)
- When you received a wedding gift, including where it was purchased, if available

- When you sent a "Thank You" note
- Was this individual invited to a shower? Include particulars
- When you received a response to the shower invitation (include particulars, if any)
- Shower gift particulars, including where it was purchased
- When you sent a "Thank You" note for the shower gift
- If the guest is from the bride's side, groom's side, or both

Then file the index card alphabetically using alphabetic dividers in a card box.

What to Wear?

I used to spend at least 20 minutes in the morning deciding what clothes to wear. I am not a morning person so those 20 minutes were precious to me and enough incentive to "become organized" in this area. I found that I not only did not know what to wear, but I was tired of the same "combination" of clothes (same shirt with the same skirt). I came up with a scheme. There are many levels to this scheme and you will need to decide what is right for you. The solution provides a quick way to choose an outfit for the day, cycling through all my clothes, and a variety of "combinations" at my fingertips. Here's how:

Organize

1. Physically separate your clothes into categories: pants, skirts, suits, shorts, dresses, blazers, tops and blouses/shirts.

2. Use an index card for each pair of pants, skirt, suit, short and dress. Write a unique description of the garment on the top left-hand side of the index card. Try to be consistent in naming of each item. Use terms such as "short sleeved shirt" to represent a shirt with buttons and short sleeves or "short sleeved top" to represent a pullover shirt. Choose meaningful words such as "Capri" or "leggings" when describing the garment.

You can take a short cut with this step. If you have a long denim skirt and a short denim skirt, you can use one card to describe both since, in most cases, the shirts/tops you choose will be the same. I found this true with not only denim, but khaki colored clothes (shorts and pants and even skirts).

3. On the top right-hand side of the index card, indicate what season(s) you wear the garment (Sp, Su, W, F). Place the dominant season first in the list, if the garment is worn in multiple seasons.
4. For each pair of pants, skirt, short and suit, go through all your blouses, shirts, tops, blazers, and sweaters and write down on the corresponding index card which of those goes with the particular pants or skirt. You will find that the index card contains several "outfits." You can also add a color on the list that would compliment the pant/skirt or suit. For example, I have a sky blue pair of pants and I know anything in *pale yellow* would compliment the pants.

5. When you are done "creating outfits," sort your index cards by dominant season.
6. *Maintenance Mode:* Every time you buy a new shirt, blouse, top, sweater, or blazer, quickly match it with all appropriate pairs of pants, shorts, suits, and skirts. Then update the index card for that item. And, don't forget to create a new index card for a new pair of pants, skirt, suit, shorts or dress.

These six steps provide a quick way of choosing an outfit in the morning. If it is the summer season, place together all index cards that have Summer defined as a season. In the morning, just choose an "index card" to wear.

Recycling

To cycle through your clothes—meaning, let's wear everything at least once before repeating (that's the extreme case)—a few more steps are required. You need to organize your closet.

1. Hang up all your blouses/shirt together, your blazers together, and your dresses together.
2. Designate one end of each grouping as an *end* (i.e. the right side or left side of the group). The end will be defined as the most recently worn garment.
3. As you decide what index card to where, look for a blouse/shirt, dress, or blazer from the *beginning* of the group; a blouse/shirt, dress, or blazer that you have not worn in awhile.

4. Once you have worn the outfit, place the blouse/shirt at the *end* of the group and place the index card behind the others (this way you are cycling through the pants/skirts as well).
5. If someone compliments you on your outfit, place an asterisk (*) next to the specific item on the index card or highlight the item. Now you'll have an idea of what outfits you really look good in! (that's great to know on a day where you need to feel good about yourself).

By cycling through your clothes, you will realize what clothes you never wear or no longer like. Take advantage of this opportunity to donate them to a charity or sell to a resale shop and reap the monetary benefits!

Don't forget to use these index cards when you shop. By seeing an index card with few items listed, you know what you need. I was in the habit of buying blouses for a favorite skirt. I had several "outfits" for that skirt, but hardly any for some "harder to match" skirts. Now you will be buying what you need instead of guessing.

These cards are a great tool when packing a suitcase. You can see what shirts are the most versatile by looking at the pants cards (or shorts or skirts) and seeing which shirts appear multiple times throughout the cards. A blue T-shirt may appear on the red pants, white jean skirt, pink shorts cards. By packing the blue T-shirt, you can create many outfits with just one shirt.

What to Wear—Kids

You certainly can carry the ideas mentioned earlier for any family member. But there is also another approach for kids. This system works well if you store clothes in the closet (not in dresser drawers). If you wish, you can put t-shirts on hangars if that's what your child wears to school. The idea behind this trick is to not wear the same shirt twice in one week. This might be a temptation for a child who is learning how to dress himself.

To start this process, group all the pants together and then group all the shirts. Now, take the shirts and arrange them into short-sleeved shirts and long-sleeved shirts. If you wish, you can take the pants one step further by lining them up by alternating colors i.e. navy pants, then khaki, then black, then navy again.

Designate one end of each grouping as an *end* (i.e. the right side or left side of the group). The end will be defined as the most recently-worn garment.

For example, let's say the *beginning* is the right-side of the group and the *end* is the left-side. Now it's the first day of school. The child should take the shirt that is on the right-most side and match it with a pair of pants. After the child has worn that outfit, move both the pants and the shirt to the left-end side of the closet.

Usually people will notice if you've worn the same shirt twice in a week more than they'd notice if you wore the same pants in a week. Now the child can cycle through shirts and pants. On the second day of school, take the next shirt in line and match it to a pair of pants. This system makes choosing what to wear a little easier on the child because there's no requirement to keep track of what's been worn recently.

If you keep shirts in a dresser drawer then just put the shirts in piles in a row. Start from right to left, bottom to top, and use the shirts in a systematic order. Pull the bottom most shirt from the right pile and when they are done wearing it, place it on the top of the pile. You can put five shirts in a pile which will be used in a one week period of time. For the next week, you move on to the next pile.

CHAPTER 4

Pick One—Any One

This section contains tricks that help out that little bit. Truthfully, if you choose just a few, you'll feel better about yourself and what you can accomplish thus bringing you some joy in your life. Some ideas are very straightforward and you'll wonder why you didn't think of that earlier. The world truly bombards us with so many things that it is just a challenge to get even the simplest things done.

Address Book

Whether you have a paper copy or electronic copy, the type of information that you include in your address book is what is important. Try writing down the names of your friends' children and the month/year of their birth, in your address book. A recommended spot is where the area codes are usually placed (especially if they are local people with the same area code as you). You can move the area code down into the number spot. So, when you're writing your Christmas cards, or those yearly Birthday cards, you can reference your friend's children at a glance.

Also, write down the email address next to their address. Your address book will become a one spot location for all information.

Backyard Pool

Do your kids ever want to go swimming in the kiddy pool at the last minute? And oooh, that water is cold. If you don't get a chance to put water in the pool in the morning (to warm up throughout the day), try this little trick: take your garden hose and unwind it so that it is in the sun. Then, fill the garden hose with water. Wait about 15 minutes and then empty the water into the kiddy pool. The sun has naturally warmed that water and rather quickly, too, I might add! Repeat the process as many times as you can. It beats running back and forth into the house with a pot of hot water!

Bag of Toys in the Car

If you have children, it is a must to keep a bag of toys in the car. Keep them either in a backpack or a cloth bag. Keep *these* toys only in the car. This way, when you go to a restaurant, bring in the toys. They will "appear" to be new toys to the kids, not a part of their every day routine. They will actually play with them longer than usual. Take the bag wherever you may need it: doctor's office, or unexpected trips.

On the same line of thought, place a basket of toys in your bedroom or any other room you want to spend time in. The kids will play with that basket of toys while you shower or get ready. That way, you aren't dragging toys from room to room and the "newness" of the toys is important.

Baskets

Somehow, I end up with a collection of baskets and I am never sure how to use them. Here are a few ideas.

- Place indoor plants inside the baskets. This idea is great for flowering plants and you can give them away as a gift.
- Roll a few of your hand towels inside the basket and use in your guest bathroom.
- Mail holder—this is a great idea for processing mail. When the mail comes in, place everything in the basket. Then take out the pieces you need to process first; the rest can wait. This way you won't have mail all over the house.
- Christmas card holder.
- Serving food: for example bread, rolls, desserts / cookies. This also makes a great gift idea if you are bringing food to a neighbor or friend.
- Cosmetics—place the cosmetics you use the most in a small basket and place on top of your bathroom counter. The items are quickly available every day.
- Place a basket on the stairs, either upstairs or downstairs (or both?). As "things" move between floors, place them in this basket to bring up/ down the next time you go. I find this particularly useful for little toys that traverse the floors of the house.

- Toy baskets—depending what size you have. I keep a "small" basket of toys in my bedroom. When I need to get ready in the morning, the kids play with those toys.
- Paper and pencil holders.
- Baby Memoirs—keep all your Welcome cards or mementos in a basket. I started at birth and have stored their id bracelets, welcome cards, cards from flowers etc. I've kept one for up to 3 years of my child's life. You can also place their birthday cards in it, and even little drawings they have done.
- Candy—each child has their own candy basket. When they deserve a treat, they go there and pick one piece of candy. Or, one LARGE combined candy basket!
- Books—place a basket of books in your family room or each bedroom. You can switch the books so there is always a variety.
- CDs/DVDs—either music, movies, or games. Place the most popular ones in a basket.
- Tapes—either VHS or cassette. Here, too, you can place the most popular ones in a basket.
- Lunch preparation—if you have to make lunches for you kids, go ahead and pack up the chips, cookies, whatever nonperishable items you can pack for the week and place them in a basket on your counter or in a cabinet. When you make their lunch (or when they make their lunch), everything is easy to get to and at your finger tips.

- Tea bags—take the tea bags out of the box and place in a nice basket. Then when you're ready for tea or you'd like to serve some to your company, bring out the basket and have a cute variety ready to choose from.

Batteries

What a surprising topic? Yes, batteries. Two ideas are listed here. If you have toys or tools that require plug in adapters/ batteries/plugs for computers, identify them! This can be done either with a piece of masking tape by writing the toy or tools name on the tape or with a permanent marker and writing right on the adapter itself. I cannot tell you how many times I find these adapters lying around and have no clue what they go to. And with the specifications per adapter, it wouldn't be wise to use it for the wrong tool or toy! For computer plugs, I have USB plugs for several cameras or other devices. I have a tag on each of them so I know which one to use to connect my device. This is especially helpful for the plug that isn't used all that often.

The second idea will save you money in buying batteries. I had the notion that for every toy or tool that required batteries, it was necessary to have the battery in the object at all times. Well, that can get expensive and frustrating when that toy is hardly played with yet the batteries are dead from just being in the toy over time. Here is a suggestion: in the area where most toys or tools are, have a box that contains several types of batteries and screwdrivers. When each toy or tool is needed, only THEN add the batteries to it.

Birthday Party List

I have hosted several birthday parties for my kids. And with repetition, I have finally learned to create a Birthday Party List of what to bring to the party. I make a copy of this list for each party and highlight or check off what I have "packed" in order to be prepared for the party. Here is a start to the list:

Balloons/Decorations/Tape/Scissors
Cake or cupcakes, ice cream
Camera, extra film or video tapes, battery
Candles, matches, lighter
Coloring sheets and markers
Cups
Drinks (juice boxes, Kool-aid, plastic bottles, water, milk)
Forks or spoons (ice cream?)
Games
Goodie bags
Invitation list (check off as kids arrive)
Napkins
Paper and pen to write gifts down
Party hats/ favors
Plastic Table clothes (usually more than 1)
Plates, 2 sizes (pizza, cake)
Serving utensil for cake, ice cream
Special plate for cake?
Wipes or liquid soap

Business Card Holder

It really is a good idea to keep a roll-a-deck/business card holder where you keep business cards of places you like. I finally found someone to help out with yard work. I took their business card and made some notes on the back of it. For example, what type of work they did for me and what I liked or didn't like about the company. I also wrote down the person who referred me to the vendor. I then filed the card under "L" for "landscape" and placed it in the card holder. Now next year, I won't have to think as hard and simply look under "landscaping" and I'll have the number to call.

If you end up not getting a business card from the vendor, you can take an old business card (it's good to keep a few old ones around) and on the back of them, create a new card with the pertinent information of what you want to store. If there is a specialty doctor that you like but didn't grab their card, write the information down any old card and file it the appropriate place in the alphabet.

Camping List

We are not big campers thus the once a year activity takes a lot of thinking! Here is a sample list of camping gear you should consider packing.

Back pack (for day trips)
Balls (football, baseball and glove, soccer)
Bathing suits and towels
Batteries
Bug spray
Canopy Tent
Coffee Maker (camping type)
Cooler (ice!)
Extension cords

Fanny pack (waist bag)
Fire pit (wood, lighter)
Fishing poles, tackle box, and bait (worms)
Flashlights
Food/Beverages (cereal, hot dogs, buns, milk, juice, pop, water, grapes, bread, peanut butter, bananas, breakfast bars)
Frisbee
Grills (propane, coal, lighters)
Lanterns
Matches or a lighter
Medicine (Aspirin, Benedril, cortozone)
Pans for cooking
Plastic plates and silverware
Radio
Rain Gear
Sleeping Bags for each person
Spare clothes
Sun glasses
Tent
Toilet paper, paper towels

Cards

This may seem like I'm stating the obvious, but buy a year's worth of cards up front. You know who you regularly send cards to each year. The next time you are at your local department store, take an extra minute NOW and buy for the year. I don't know how many times I have delayed in sending a card because I don't have the special "Happy Birthday to my Aunt" card and I don't always make the time to run out at the (very) last minute.

Catalogs, Storage of

I do keep around some catalog although I have paired down the mailings quite a bit (a few toll-free calls and asking them to take me off their mailing list). The ones I do keep, I have a stack on a bookshelf. You could also use a nice basket to store them. The idea is to always add the most recent catalogs to the top of the pile. When the pile gets too high, and in my case, that means when it hits the next shelf, throw away the old catalogs from the bottom of the pile. You can remove maybe a third of the pile, or at most a half of the pile. That should allow you to keep at least one copy of the catalogs that you like. If you have some catalogs that you want to keep for a longer period of time, put them in a different place so they don't get accidentally removed in the cycle.

Chapped Lips

Sometimes the winter months can be brutal on the good ol' lips. Each of us (family members) has their own lip ointment to help in this time. But, they are all the same brand ... hmmm, whose is whose??? And we don't want to use someone else's. A simple solution is to wrap a piece of masking tape around each stick and place the family member's initials on it. This is a better solution than buying different brands or flavors per family member ... the memory of who's is who's isn't that great.

Children's Behavior

Yes, even children's' behavior can be organized. Well, a little! I needed a mechanism to show my children how often they were saying unkind words or doing unkind deeds. I was frustrated at nagging so I came up with a simple solution. Show them. Create a chart with the names of your children on it. Then place this chart in a well-viewed area like a refrigerator door. Tell them that any time they say or do something kind, they will get a plus sign (+) on the chart. And, any time they say or do something unkind, they will get a minus sign (-). Then, attach a reward or something at the end of it once they reach a certain goal. Make sure you are consistent with placing the appropriate mark on the chart. You may be amazed, the chart may not be needed but the children will get in the habit of asking if they get a plus for their good behavior.

Another avenue to demonstrate to the children about their behavior is to hand out "tickets." I created "interrupt," "bad words" (the use of stupid, idiot etc.), and "complaining" tickets. I set aside a cup for each child and placed the appropriate ticket in their cup. If they ended up with 3 tickets, I had them write a verse from the Bible on the appropriate subject!

Children's Birthday Lists

Whenever my kids see or hear of something they'd like to have, I have them write it down on a special piece of paper (or index card) entitled "Birthday List for —" (child's name). As time goes on, they write down what they think they would like for their birthday. They can review this list and edit it as they choose. It makes them think of what they'd like and really think twice about it. Then when it comes time for their birthday, you won't have to guess at what they like. Again, you're spending your dollars wisely on something you know that they would enjoy.

And you can share this list with the family members (grandparents, aunts/uncles). If you do share this list, write down the family member's initials next to the gift idea so you don't hand it out more than once.

You can also keep this list in the "Little Spiral Notebook" described in Chapter 1.

Children's Communication

This idea is easy and no real preparation is necessary. Some children are just not talkers. They can be away from you at school or playing at someone's house and when they return, you still aren't sure if they had a good time or not! In a quiet moment or at bedtime, just ask them a few questions: What made you happy today? What made you sad today? What made you laugh today? What made you angry today? Be prepared to share answers about your day! You may be amazed at what answers you get!

Children's Craft Box

We all like our children to get involved with projects. To make this simple, find or buy a storage box, say 12-qt size or so. Place your crayons, markers, stamps, stickers etc. in this box. (I put all the stickers in a zip lock baggie, and all the craft items i.e. pipe cleaners, felt, pom poms etc. in another large zip-lock baggie.) Place just enough in the box to keep a child busy. For example, if you have 100 markers, place only 20 or so in the box. Put the other 80 in another box, out of sight. When the original 20 markers start to run dry, grab some replacements from the box. This way, the child isn't overwhelmed, you're not picking up millions of markers during clean up time, and you're not always running out to the store to buy new. You'll have your own store of spares at your disposal. The same idea works for coloring books. Place just a few coloring books in the craft box. Make sure the child completes a coloring book before adding a new one. Why waste paper and money by having a child work in several coloring books at one time and never finishing a one? I am not into spending a lot of time in cleanup—whether it's the child doing it or me!

As an aside, kids love to work with or "create with" wrapping paper tubes, paper towel tubes or toilet paper tubes. Anytime you come across one of these, throw it in a designated paper bag. It may seem that they accumulate rather fast, but one child's art project can empty it very quickly!

Children's Journal

One of the best gifts you can give to your child is a story about them. It is easy to create a journal for your child. In the journal, you can write about special things that happened that day or week. Start by buy a spiral notebook for each of your children. I prefer the shorter, thicker spiral notebooks instead of the 8½x11 inch ones. Keep the journal(s) by your bed. Then right before you go to bed, if there is something you'd like to capture about the day, quickly jot it down in the child's journal. Or, if a thought comes to you in the middle of the day, and you know you want to include it, write a note to yourself (sometimes I put this on my "This Week's List" from Chapter 1) and make sure you have it at bedtime. Don't feel over-whelmed that you must write in the journal every day. Certainly a week can go by (or even a month) but if you can capture some of their happy times, sad times, funny sayings, the book will be cherished by everyone.

And as you capture the child's "first" i.e. lost their first tooth, or took their first step, or first day of school, highlight the word "first" and the next key word (tooth, step, school) with a highlighter and you'll create a quick list of "first" at a glance.

Children's Memorabilia, School/Art Work

If you have children that are in any sort of school (preschool, park district classes, grade school etc.), you know how much "art" they bring home. It can get overwhelming with just one school age child, let alone more than one. Having grown up without many tangible items from my past, I think it's important to keep a few pieces of "art work" or other collectable items for a child. I have a three-step system that is easy. My example will be for one child, but just duplicate the supplies for each child.

There is some setup for this system. First, you'll need to purchase a stackable sorter (plastic holder that hold 8½x11 pieces of paper). This is the "art work" stackable sorter.

Then you'll need two types of cardboard, dresser-like boxes. Purchase one small dresser box with four drawers and a second, wider box with six drawers (shorter and wider than the first).

Label the drawers in the six-drawer box with ascending ages. I suggest Kindergarten, First Grade, etc.

Label each drawer in the four-drawer box to hold various "items." For example, Cards (i.e. birth announcements, birthdays), Souvenirs, Medical History, Pictures, etc. You may combine these labels or simply have one for each drawer (your decision may depend on how many kids you have).

You'll also need a manila file folder labeled "School—Needs Action" and a brown paper bag.

Now, when you're child brings home artwork, you can store it right away because you're organized! As you empty your child's school backpack, look through the papers and sort them. Pull the "Need Action" papers and place in the file folder. Remove a few art pieces you want to keep and place them in the "art work" stackable sorter. Take any souvenirs, cards, etc. and file them in the four-drawer dresser.

Put everything else in the brown paper bag. This is important. Keep the bag in another room or somewhere inconspicuous. Later, if your child asks for a particular piece of art or school work, you can easily retrieve it. If your child never asks for the artwork then, when the bag is full, throw it away and start a new bag.

When the art work stacker is full, then "empty" it into the age-appropriate art-work drawer(s) of the six-drawer box. When your child receives cards, medical documents, etc., place them in the four-drawer box immediately.

You may alter the way you use the four-drawer box. Purchase another stackable sorter and use that as the interim storage location. When it's full, then empty it and sort the contents into one of the four drawers.

Since I have three kids, I have six stackers, 3x3, side by side, and the large, six-drawer box together in one room. The four-drawer dresser is in the basement because the stackable storage tray doesn't fill up that fast. One set of three is used for souvenirs and cards and the other set is used for art and school work.

You can also place the Medical History in the Medical Information folder (see Chapter 1, "File Drawers" section).

Children's Shoes

A great container to keep children's shoes in is the cardboard boxes that hold 8½ x11 papers from the office supply store. These boxes are about 17½ inches deep by 12 inches wide, by 9½ inches in height. You could use a plastic tub about a similar size, but they are rather expensive and they are going to get a lot of abuse. You can use one paper box per child. This idea usually works well for children 10 and under, or until their shoes get too big for the box!

Children's Teeth

What? Children's Teeth? Do you try desperately to keep up with your child's baby book? The first year may have entries, but they expect you to keep adding to it, especially the pages designated for "teeth history." I am guilty of "not keeping up" but I do think keeping track of losing a tooth is fun. So my short cut is to just take a picture, with a camera that prints the date on the picture, on the day my child has lost their tooth. I have them give me a great big smile, and I snap the picture. When the picture is printed, I write down what tooth is missing (in case it is not apparent from the picture) and place it in the child's baby book. This way, I don't have to put my memory to the test … the camera did it for me!

Children's Yearly Portraits

Do you happen to collect a portrait of each child each year of their life? In the first 2 years of our children's life, we took pictures (8x10, wallets etc.) at the local portrait place every six months (they are adorable pictures, of course!). And after that, we continue the "tradition" on a yearly basis. After awhile, these pictures add up and I wasn't sure what to do with them. So I created a special "Portrait Photo Album" to store these memories. I chose a photo album where I can add pages and that have the "pocket sleeve" pages. I started the album with my oldest child's pictures and labeled each page with the age of the picture, earliest to 18 years of age. Then I started the next child's pages after that, earliest to age 18 etc. I file all the "extra" wallet pictures or portrait pictures in these sleeved pages. I also file the 8x10 picture of the previous year when I replace it (on the wall) with the most current picture in the wall picture frame. Now I have "one stop shopping" to see the changes in my children throughout their years. And, it is very hard for me to even throw away one of these precious trinkets to I just file them all!

Chores—the Simple Ones

Use your calendar to remind you of some of the simple chores you do. For instance, every Friday, change your towels. Every 15th and 30th, change the sheets on the beds. Whatever routine chores you do, try to make it easy to remember by tying them to a repetitive time frame. You can expand this to include "shopping" or "cleaning." I found that if I dedicate every Wednesday to go grocery shopping, my shopping list is complete and my expectations are set. Without dedicating a day, I was running errands "haphazardly" and this was not efficient. I spent more time in the car than I had to.

Christmas Cards

A down and dirty tracking for Christmas cards is this simple. As you send a Christmas card to someone, write down the last two digits of the current year in your address book.

Then, if they send you a Christmas card, underline the last two digits of the year. If they send you a card and you have not yet sent one, you'll see just an underline in your address book. This is a good reminder of whom you still need to send a card to. You can do the same even on an electronic list.

Christmas Decorations

Sometimes the simplest ideas escape me. If this sounds too obvious, forgive me, but it took me a few years to figure this one out. When Christmas time came around, I really wanted to decorate my house with all the Christmas knick-knacks, but I become frustrated due to the lack of space. My tables and shelves already had decorations on them and didn't spare much room for more. To solve that problem, get a new box or use your Christmas decoration box, and take down some of the "ordinary" decorations and place them in the box. Now there is room for the Christmas decorations. And, you won't loose track of where the "ordinary" decorations are. When Christmas is over, the "ordinary" decorations will all be in the box, waiting to return to their home.

Christmas Decorations, Storage

We start decorating for Christmas as early as right after Thanksgiving. We usually bring out all of our boxes and start to unpack them. I have noticed that it is a lot simpler if we store our decorations in the following manner:

Box 1: lights for outdoors

Box 2: all decorations for the Christmas tree (including lights, and ornaments)

Box 3: Christmas decorations

Box 4: Winter decorations (ones that stay up longer than just Christmas, for instance, snowmen decorations

When we did this, I could take out the box that I needed at the right time. We may put up our outdoor Christmas lights sooner than we setup our tree. And we may decorate our tree before I am able to put up the Christmas decorations. The winter decorations last longer than the Christmas so it's nice to have a box just for them so all of the Christmas boxes are back in the basement but the winter box remains.

Christmas or Holiday Shopping

Here's yet another use for the "Little Spiral Notebook," from Chapter 1. About a month or so before the holidays, write down each person you have to buy a gift for on a page of the notebook. Use one line for one person (thus a page will have several names listed). This will allow you to see who you would like to buy gifts for and who is missing! All the names will be in one spot. Next to the name, write in the gift you'd like to buy. As you actually buy the gift, highlight that person's name. That will denote that you're "done" shopping for that person. By putting this information in the "Little Spiral Notebook," you'll have it with you at all times.

Christmas Ornaments, Storage

I always thought it was a challenge to store the Christmas ornaments. I liked the idea of the special plastic storage containers that you could buy at the store, but they are so big and really don't hold enough ornaments for the amount of space the box takes up. So, I came up with another idea. Take a sturdy clothing box about 3-5 inches deep, and 14-20 inches long. The sturdier the cardboard clothes box, the better.

Then get a supply of the packing "popcorn" used in shipping (usually a box that you receive in the mail from any store will contain this, especially if you have ordered fragile things). As you pack your ornaments, put the flat ones on the bottom of the clothes box. Cover the bottom of the box with as many ornaments as you can without overlapping them. Once the bottom is covered, put a layer of packing "popcorn" on top of the ornaments. Add another layer of ornaments. Layer more packing "popcorn." A clothes box should be able to handle about 3 layers of ornaments. Then start another box.

If you have many glass-bulb type ornaments, use a deeper box, 8-10 inches or so square (a gift box of some sort). Use generous quantities of tissue paper to separate the glass ornaments from each other.

If you reach the point of having too many ornaments to decorate one tree, then add a note card or blank sticker to each ornament box. Select a few boxes to use for decorating the tree and write the current year on the sticker or card. Rotate boxes of ornaments by choosing a box that doesn't have the last year's date on it.

This topic has several flavors to it. In addition, you could store your ornaments by year they were received or by child who receives them. Each year, we receive about 20 new ornaments (including the beloved hand made ones from our children). I have a Christmas spiral notebook where I include special memories about each Christmas (the type of tree, a synopsis of Christmas Eve and Christmas day memories) including a description of the new ornaments we received that year and who we received them from. I have also tried to label the ornament with the year it was received if at all possible (and in good taste). You could label one of the clothes box with the current year and start placing the new ornaments in the box (have your packing "popcorn" on hand!). Even if the year isn't important to you, having a new box ready for these special gifts makes "clean up" time just a little easier.

Or, you could provide a box with each of your children's names on it. As ornaments are received throughout the year for each person, you could write their first initial on the ornament (along with the year) and store ornament according to "whose it is." This box of ornaments becomes special to the child and, when the child is ready to leave the "nest," they have some ornaments to take with them to decorate their own tree. And, they also look forward to decorating the tree with their special ornaments.

As an aside, it is a fun tradition to give each of your children a special ornament (maybe start this tradition at their birth) that they hang on the tree every year. They really do look forward to hanging it on the tree. It makes them feel special (and they are!).

Christmas Presents

Do you ever get frustrated at having thrown out a receipt or instruction to a new Christmas "gadget" or toy? Usually there is a lot of commotion as Christmas presents are opened. To avoid that frustration and any that may occur later, have a slash folder with you whenever you open presents. As soon as there is something of importance (gift receipt or instructions), place it in the slash folder. I have mine handy for a few weeks after Christmas so as we play with the toys, I know what the rules are, quickly!

To take this one step further, keep a pencil handy and quickly right whom the gift is from as you place the paper in the slash folder.

Computer Organization

In this day and age, we need some organization around our computer. Here are three ideas for a start. It seems like every web site wants you to have a user name and password. This can be overwhelming to keep track of. I suggest keeping a small spiral notebook by your computer work area and inside, list the website, user name and password. It is easiest if you label each page with a letter of the alphabet. Then write the website, username and password. For example, under A (the first page) you may list AMAZON.COM and your login information. You may want to keep only "less sensitive" passwords here like the ones used for shopping or sending gift baskets. You could use another spiral notebook for more important passwords but keep it with you or hide it well.

The second idea comes from a bad experience … my disk drive failed. The good news is that I had a pretty good backup of my data, but I didn't have a good backup of all the software I had installed on the computer. What I realized is that I didn't have a good idea of what software was important to me to rebuild the computer. I now have an index card that lists the software that is vital to my computer work habits. I also have a shoe box that contains the CDs that go with the index card. Should this happen again, and I certainly hope not, I know right where to go to reinstall the software. Lesson learned: backup your computer either via the backup tool or copying files to a thumb drive (USB storage device).

The last idea is used when you first purchase your computer. Quickly get out a plastic bag (I prefer the 1 gallon freezer bags with a zip lock) and place everything that comes with the computer, in it! This includes CDs, manuals, wires, adapters … everything. Then simply label the bag with the computer name or unique identifier should you have more than one computer. In case of an emergency should you ever need to rebuild your computer (due to a disk crash!), you'll have what you need in a moment's notice.

Donations, Cash or Credit

If you use checks as your means of donating money, highlight each donation check entry in your check register with a highlighter as you write it. Then, at the year's end, when it is time to calculate the amount of donations, it is easy enough to add up the highlighted entries in your checkbook register. You can use this mechanism, along with any donation receipts (keep in a separate envelope i.e. Contributions) to provide that dollar amount to Uncle Sam. It is easy to make sure each check register entry has a donation receipt and if for some chance, you have lost the donation receipt, you'll have a reminder of what you actually spent.

If you use a credit card for your donations, then highlight the item on your credit card statement. You can go through these at the end of the year and add up the highlighted items as well. Or, you can make an entry in your check register noting the name and amount but enclosing it inside of parenthesis. Leave the DEDUCT column in the check register blank. With this method, you only have to look in one place for your donations.

If you happen to donate to organizations that are not "not-for-profit" but can't always remember which ones are and are not, write a list on the front of the Contribution envelope that you use to store the receipts. Write the name of the organization (or abbreviation) and a simple "yes" to indicate it is a tax deduction or "no" that it is NOT a tax deduction.

Donations, Clothing, Toys, etc.

To assist you in getting your house "clutter free" and to really help others that can use those items, set aside a brown paper bag in your closet or bedroom. Keep a piece of paper and pen in the bag or by the bag. Every time you want to donate an object, place it in the bag and write the item down on the piece of paper. This is really easy as you try on some clothes and decide they don't fit or you don't like them anymore. Or, as the kids outgrow something just throw it in the bag. Keep doing this until several bags are full. When AMVETS or Salvation Army calls you to see if you have anything to donate, you'll be all ready.

Dry Cleaner Plastic Bags

What a title. If you use dry cleaning services at all, re-use the plastic bags for your own clothes. If there are "odd season" clothes that you wear only every other 6 months, store them in these bags. Or, any "work clothes" or "formal clothes" that are worn only occasionally. Your clothes will be clean when it's time to wear them. The alternative is dust on the shoulders!

Ear Plugs?

I found a pair and was about to throw them away when I had a thought ... we recently went to the fireworks and parades for the 4th of July and my kids kept covering their ears. The noise was just too loud for these little ears. This would have been a great place to bring ear plugs! They could enjoy the event without covering their ears the whole time.

Extra Clothes in the Car

Here is another simple trick and has proven itself valuable each and every time. Keep some spare clothes in your car for each child. For example, have a shirt, pants, underwear, socks and sweatshirt for each child and store them in a duffle bag. Remember to make the clothes appropriate for the season that you're in. This comes in handy when they accidentally get muddy, or rained upon, or sick, and even, when they just need an extra layer of clothes for that extra cold soccer game that you all are watching!

Fast Food Coupons

Clip them and store them. But where? In your car. Anywhere in your car: the glove compartment, a side pocket, or even in a slash folder underneath your seat. I can't tell you home many times I've stored them at home and then decide, as I am out and about, that I don't have any thing planned for dinner, I should stop and pick up fast food. But where are my coupons? At home. Not good. If you place them in your car, you'll have them readily available WHEN you need them! This idea is also good for coupon books (the ones that are for local establishments). These books should be kept in your car.

Games (Instructions for)

Are you tired of losing instructions for games? Usually, you can memorize the rules, but not always. If the instructions come on a separate piece of paper (as oppose to on the lid of the box), take the paper and store it in a three-ring binder. Put all of your instructions there and better yet, file them alphabetically by the name of the game. You won't have to refer to it often but when you do, it's a "non-issue."

This is a good idea for Lego maps/instructions as well. These don't always fit perfectly into a three-ring binder, but do the best with what you have. Otherwise, the pages get ripped, separated, lost ... need I say more? Another idea would be to store all the "Lego-type" maps in a plastic Tupperware container.

Gifts on Hand

Have you ever been caught off guard and needed a gift? It could be for a teacher, or a house warming gift or a friend of your child's birthday party. I have a designated area to store "extra" gifts and use these when I am in a panic! If you can, set aside a small place in your home, maybe a part of a closet, as a designated "gifts on hand" area. The next you find a great sale on an item you think would be great as a gift, buy it and place it in this area. Or sometimes a child receives so many gifts or duplicate gifts that they can be placed in this area for someone else to use some day. Or, and we have to admit this, sometimes we receive a gift that isn't quite "us" and it can go in that space, too. If you ever go to "home" parties (for candles, home decorations etc.) and you want to buy something but not a lot (and you don't really need anything more), choose one item to buy as a gift for someone and store it in this space.

This really works for after-Christmas sales. I found some great Christmas pillows that I want to give to the Sunday school teachers for the following Christmas (at 90% off the original price).

Guest Book

This idea is just for fun. We had a Wedding Guest book when we were first married. It seemed a shame that some many pages were left blank. So we turned it into a House Guest book as well. Now, when anyone visits us for an overnight stay, we have them "register' in our Guest Book. They write the date of their stay, their signature and any comments they may want to make. It's great to see who has visited over a long period of time, or even how many guests you have in one year. And, of course, you can choose any guest book to use; it can be brand new.

Hand-Me-Downs

Are shoes included in the hand me down list? If so, buy a shoe holder that goes in your closet. It holds at least 10 pairs of shoes. Place all the hand me down shoes in the holder—starting at the top with the smallest shoe size. Then, label the shoe compartment with a sticky label or something, to show the shoe size. This reminds you what you already have and don't need to buy. Sometimes I panic and think I need to buy shoes as my kids are growing out of their old ones, but I first search the closet shoe hangar before I go shopping.

If you receive hand-me-down clothes that are too big for your kids at this point, then find a small box or a brown paper bag and sort the clothes by size and even season, if you can. Label the outside of the box or bag. You may end of with a Size 10, Summer or a Size 5 Winter. If you have the space, keep these in the child's closet, on the floor or tucked away somewhere. Or, keep the bag or box in a basement but in full view. The idea is that the box or bag should be in view so you remember you have clothes. This should curb any impulse buying you may have (thinking that you don't have any clothes for that size!).

Health–Keeping Track

This subject should get more attention than it does. You should implement this tid-bit for each person in your family. Create a file folder with the title of "Health." Then take a sheet of paper for each member in your family. Divide each paper into four columns then label each column as follows: Start Date, End Date, Symptoms, Saw Doctor? Have this folder in a very handy place for easy access. Any time some one gets sick, even just the sniffles, write it on their Health sheet and fill in the columns. This sheet may ultimately detect if there is a repeating illness, i.e. allergies or asthma. Or, it may show that you are a very healthy family and keep up the good work!

For this folder, I'd suggest you keep it very handy. In Chapter 1, "File Drawer" section, I recommend a "frequently used" file holder. You should place this medical folder in that holder.

Important Dates List

Time passes by so quickly; I don't always get a chance to remember what day it is or whose birthday is in this month. If you're not yet storing these dates in an electronic calendar system, then create for yourself a list of important dates (you can create this on the computer). Organize it by month, then sequential dates. Write down each important date, and add the year of the occasion in parenthesis ( ). For example, FEBRUARY: 2 — Rhonda's birthday ('64), 22 -Mom/Dad's anniversary ('45). These dates can be store on a sheet of paper or on index cards, 1 card per month.

And, for each important date that you are planning to send a card, circle those dates on your yearly calendar. When you are looking at your calendar, you will quickly know what dates are coming up and to send a card.

Internet Addresses

With the age of the Internet, it is really important to know how to store a personal Internet directory. Create a spreadsheet with 3 columns: site address, Category, and notes. Every time you read or hear about an Internet site that you may be interested in, place it in the spreadsheet. The key is to standardize on the categories so you can sort them.

Sample categories include:

Airlines
Auctions
Auto Sales
Cell phone services
Clothes
Computer Sales
Congress
Coupons
Coupons, grocery
Coupons, local
Flowers
Food

- Fraud
- Furniture
- Gardening
- Government
- Home Sales
- Hotels
- Internet Providers
- Jobs
- Libraries
- Magazines
- Mortgages
- New Homes
- Newspapers
- Schools
- Shopping
- Shopping, baby
- Shopping, clothes
- Shopping. designers
- Shopping, electronics
- Stocks
- Toys
- Travel
- Used Cars
- Web directories

So the next time you're looking at buying a DVD player, look at the sites under the "shopping, electronics" category.

Internet Credit Card

To limit credit card fraud, use a separate credit card (number) for all of your internet purchases. For years, we had only one credit card that we used for everything. Then when discussing "what if" something happened with Internet fraud, we started to think of what a royal pain that would be to cancel that card and start anew. So we applied for a new credit card (no annual fee, if you can!) and use that one only for Internet purchases.

You may also want to visit Chapter 3, "Internet Shopping" section, for other tricks regarding internet shopping.

Internet Favorites Folder

In addition to or as an alternative, use the "Favorite Folders" option in your Internet Browser. Again, the key to success here is to have the correct categories or folders. Some suggestions are:

Clothing: Do you have favorite sites where you like to go for online clothes shopping? List them here. I have to buy polo shirts for my boys for their school dress code and I list five sites where I normally buy from and do a little bit of price comparison when it comes time to purchase.

Compare Shopping: Sites that help you find the best price i.e. Bizrate.com or Froogle.com.

Cooking: There are so many sites that offer recipes. I group them here.

Coupons: Sites where you can find coupons for local establishments on-line.

Entertainment: List theater web sites, restaurants or dining web sites, movie theater tickets

Family Concerns: I mark my local church's web site, or citizen action groups that I participate in. I have a "Movie Review" web site that I list here as well. McGruff.com is also a good site (information on protecting your child from bullys).

Family Fun: Anytime you see something that you're family can do, mark it here. This includes local entertainment (maybe a water park where you want to know its hours of operation).

Hobbies (name them): I enjoy knitting and scrap booking. I mark sites that pertain to these hobbies under a "knitting" and "scrap book" folder.

Local: Park Districts, Village web site, nearby city's web site.

News: What sites do you like to read for the latest news?

Research (be specific): If you are about to buy something, I would recommend using the web for research on the product. For instance, if you are looking for a digital camera, there are several sites that will review them for you. You can bookmark these sites under "Camera Research."

Sports: Is your family active in any sports? Place all the web site information in this folder.

Vacation (be specific): If you're planning a trip, use the web to research the location and store that information here. Visitor bureau sites, or City Tickets sites can have many ideas of what to do while in town.

Junk Box

Have one! You can use a shoe box for this and any time you come across something that you are not sure what it is, place it in this box. Sometimes I find pieces of "things" and I am not sure what they are but they look important and I don't want to throw them away … yet. I place them in this box. This box then is the first place I look when I find out a piece is missing from a tool or device.

Kitchen Rug

I have a kitchen rug in front of my sink. It is probably the most used rug in my house and you can tell by how it looks. I was rather embarrassed by this rug—no matter how hard I tried, I just couldn't get it cleaned and when I was entertaining, well, I didn't like it. So I decided to go and get a relatively "cheap" rug that is "easy" to clean and use it ONLY when I entertain. After I am done preparing for my company, I swap out the old well-used rug for my nice clean rug. What a difference that makes. And you don't have to spend a lot of money on the new rug since you won't really be using it that often.

Library Bag

Have you ever lost a library book? The good news is we are bringing home more books from the library lately. The bad news is we are bringing home more books from the library lately. I have discovered that if I dedicate a duffle bag, or a canvas bag as "The Library Bag," my chances of losing a book are smaller (not impossible, though!). The rule is, take ONE book from the bag at a time and it must be returned to the bag before another is taken out. The same thing is true with DVDs, VCR movies or anything else that comes from the library. The tote bag also makes these trips to the library a little easier on the arms. I am not as clumsy with a tote bag as I am when carrying 20 lose items.

Like and Dislike

My memory is poor. There is something frustrating about not remember what is "good" and what is "bad" even just from a performance stand point. Sometimes I find cleaning brands that I like. There are so many counter top cleaners, but there is one I like in particular. Create two envelopes and label one "LIKE" and the other "DISLIKE." As you come across products, foods, wine or anything that you have purchased and are happy or sad with it, write the name on a piece of paper and place in the envelope. Or, if convenient, tear off a piece of the product's label and store in the envelope. You can bring the envelopes with you when you're shopping or quickly glance at them before you go shopping.

Another approach is to write "I LIKE IT" or a PLUS sign on the product label. Or take a piece of masking tape and place on the product then write on the tape. For example, I buy different brands of nail polish and after wearing them, I like some brands better than others. So I place a piece of masking tape over the bottle and wrote "I LIKE IT' and with the ones I didn't like, I wrote "I DON'T LIKE IT." Then I know the next time I shop for nail polish, I am aware of the brand that I like. I cannot rely on my memory any more!

This system comes in handy for over the counter medicines. Some medicines for colds or fevers, my kids will take. Or, one child likes one flavor but cannot stand another. So on the medicine label, I write the child's name and whether or not they like the medicine. I was getting tired of seeing so many "unused" medicines in my cabinets because my kids would complain so much about their taste. I want to buy only what we are going to use.

Lunch Money

Where my children go to school, "hot lunch" is provided on a per day basis. Unfortunately, the "hot lunch" items are a little pricey. My kids kept asking for hot lunch and I wasn't sure how to put a limit on it. Then I had an idea. I took an empty envelope for each child. I place a specified amount of money (say $5.00) in the envelope and wrote down the date (I did this on a Monday, purposely). I told them they can use this money any day within a two-week period. In two weeks, I'll take out any left over money, and put in another

$5.00. This way, they were accountable for their own number of times they wanted "hot lunch" and how much they wanted to spend each time they ordered. You can set your own dollar amount and I find that a two-week window did work well. They were also responsible for taking the money out of the envelope on the days they wanted "hot lunch."

Lunches

If you have to provide lunches for yourself or your children, I encourage you to make them ahead of time, for instance on Sunday evening. It is easy to make a week's worth of sandwiches, mark them (masking tape and write a name or cut them uniquely per child) and place them in the freezer. If you can buy larger packages of chips or crackers, you can place these in Baggies, again, for a week's time. I even store my baggies in a nice basket that is on the counter top. This will save money since buying pre-packaged chips is more expensive than buying just a large package. Choose fruits like whole apples, bananas, or vegetables like carrots, celery or broccoli that you can pre-cut and place in a container of water. Then, the morning of, place the vegetables in a baggy, and then grab one of everything else and place in the lunch bag. You can place the week's worth of nonperishable items in a basket to make things look neat and tidy. Your children can even help if you make an index card of what goes in a lunch (like a packing list). They can read the card and take from the piles to create their lunch.

Magazines

This is a truly simple idea and helpful. Some magazines subscriptions arrive very frequently. I start one magazine, then put it down, and before I know it, another one shows up and I am not sure if I ever finished the first one. As you complete a magazine, simply put an "X" on the front cover somewhere, maybe beside your name/address section to denote that you have finished reading this magazine. This is especially helpful if more than one person reads the magazine. And in that case, put your initials, then the "X" on the cover. You won't be re-browsing the same old magazine.

Medical/Dental Insurance Claims

Wow—I get lost when I have to keep track of health claims. So lost, I needed to do something about it. I wanted to make sure I was getting reimbursed in all cases. With this system in place, I was able to "reclaim" several hundreds of dollars that was owed to me. Fill in column one and two after each doctor's visit. Then fill in the rest of the columns as you receive the insurance claim form.

Take a piece of paper and divide it into six columns. Title each column:

Date of Service: Write down the date of the doctor appointment.

What: Write who and for what the appointment was for i.e. Jane, two-months, well-baby visit.

Net amount: Write down the actual dollar amount that is owed to the doctor (or hospital etc.). If you have a PPO, there tends to be a "list price" and a reduced "agreed upon" price. That price is what is ultimately owed to the physician.

Deductible: If you have a deductible and if payment goes towards the deductible, write the dollar amount of the payment in this column. Mark the dollar amount with a "pd" if you have already paid the physician.

I Owe: Write down the dollar amount you need to pay. Mark the dollar amount with a "pd" if you have already paid it. You can also add "cc" if you paid by credit card or "cash" if you paid with cash.

Insurance Benefit: Write down the dollar amount the insurance company paid to the physician. Fill in this column when you get an insurance statement and it states that they have paid the physician. It's also good to look back on this column over a year's time to see the benefit you've gotten from the insurance company.

I keep this piece of paper in the Medical Folder. Whenever we have a doctor or dentist visit, I place the receipt and/or bill in the folder. When the insurance form comes in, I match it up with the paperwork, staple together and file in the back of the folder. The outstanding bills remain in the front, while the complete items move to the back.

Now, there are a few variations to this tip as well. Sometimes the insurance bill has several claims on it. If your medical frequency is average, then you can staple all the bills associated with that claim form. However, if you have several bills, i.e. several hospital visits a year, you can set up monthly file folders and still staple your bill to the insurance claim and then file it in the appropriate month of the *date of service* of the medical treatment. You may find you need to make a copy of the insurance claim to represent only one month's worth of claims. To walk you through this, let's say you receive an insurance claim that has four services on it, and straddles two months. You had a hospital visit in May and three follow-up visits in June. Make a copy of the insurance claim form. Use one copy for May and staple only the appropriate billings for the hospital visit to the form. Use the other copy for June and staple the follow up visits' bills on that claim form.

Monthly Bills

As a monthly bill comes in, keep the envelope it comes in and then store the bill in the envelope. Add to the envelope each month. This way it is easy to identify what bills are where. I keep all my bill envelops in a desk drawer. At the end of the year, take each envelope and file it in a box marked TAXES for Year XXXX. Quick and easy and you know where it is!

Also, if you are able, write the checks for each bill and place it in the stamped envelope, but don't mail it yet! Write on the outside front corner of the envelope either the due date of the bill, or the date to mail it by. Keep the bills in a pile somewhere that you see each day and check if any bills need to be mailed out for that date.

As an aside, keep all your credit card receipts in an envelope or in a letter slot. Choose one location that you always visit and keep all your receipts there so when that monthly credit card bill comes in, you can make sure you're being billed for the right things. Ditto for cash, keep it in a separate envelope, in the case that you need to make a return on an item.

Necklaces and Bracelets

I like to see what necklaces and bracelets I have instead of opening jewelry boxes (hiding the jewelry). I found a tie hanger or belt hangar that really helps display each item. You need to purchase two special hangers, one for necklaces and one for bracelets. Again, by presenting these items to you in an open fashion, you're more apt to wear one without having to remember to search for one. Another variation for bracelets would be a mug stand that has six pegs. You can display your bracelets much like a department store would.

Organizing Drawers

Quite a few of my drawers were a mess! The messiest are mostly the drawers found in the bathroom, desks, etc. To help make the best use of the space, I use little boxes to create dividers or containers within the drawer. Flat boxes, about one-half- to one-inch tall, work the best (for example, check book boxes that you get when you first get your checks or a re-order). For bathroom drawers, you can use one box for your makeup, another for combs and hairbrushes, yet another for barrettes, hair ties, etc. Shoe boxes work best for underneath the sink, in a bathroom cabinet. You can pull the shoeboxes out as you need them similar to a drawer. For a desk, you can use a box or several boxes to contain pens and pencils, scissors, rubber-bands, mini pads of paper etc. Use baggies where appropriate, too, in such cases as storing rubber bands or paper clips. I even use the little check book boxes to organize my earrings. I divide up my loose earrings among three boxes so I can find the pair of earrings faster.

Photo Albums

Do you take a lot of pictures but get overwhelmed when trying to place them in an album? Consider this. Separate your pictures into "Family Events" and "per child." You can put "Family Event" photos in a main album (sorted by year?) but have individual 4x6 albums for each child to put pictures of them in their own album. As soon as you get your picture, you can separate it by "Family Event" or "per child." You can separate their albums by age (0, 1, 2 etc.). Each child can look at their album whenever they want and it will be done. The family album may take more time to create (see "Photo Organization" section for ideas in how to make that go faster).

Photo Organization

If you place your photos in any kind of album (scrap booking or just a normal album), it may get too overwhelming to continue this habit, and you may be tempted to give up. Try this trick. Get a 4x6 index card holder. As you get your prints, place them in chronological order in this card holder. If you do scrap booking, place a 4x6 index card in-between pages or occasions so you know what pictures to consider when you are ready to work on that page. You don't have to sort through the good pictures / bad pictures yet. You can do that when it is time for you to work on your album.

Photo Storage (Negatives and Digital)

If you are still using film, when you get your film developed, save the envelope that the prints comes in. On the outer upper right hand corner, write in the date range for the pictures, i.e. April 2007 — June 2007. Keep the negatives in the envelop and place it in a shoe box that is wide enough to store the photo envelope without bending it. You can also store extra prints in the same envelope. File the envelopes sequentially, starting with the oldest date in the front of the shoebox and the most recent date at the end of the shoebox. It now becomes easy to retrieve those negatives for grandma when she wants reprints of little Joey's birthday party. Ultimately, it is good to store your negatives in a fire proof box.

Digital picture storage is just as important and probably one we don't give much thought to. If you haven't had your computer break down on you yet, you are fortunate. I never thought it would happen to me, but it did. My first reaction was "Oh No! I haven't printed all my digital photos yet … Have I lost them forever?" I was blessed, and had a very recent backup of all the photos so I didn't lose any. But, my computer disk was corrupt beyond repair and without that backup, I would have lost all my photos (and everything else). If you are computer savvy, make sure you setup a backup job to backup your photos, preferably to another computer. But if you want a simple solution, purchase a large thumb drive (USB storage device), say several gigabytes in storage, and copy your digital pictures to that thumb drive. It is best to store that thumb drive in a fire proof vault (purchase at any office store) but even having it in your desk draw is better than not having it at all. You will need a good discipline of remembering to copy to that thumb drive each time you add a set of pictures to your computer but it is worth it! With the price of thumb drives becoming affordable, it is also a good idea to backup other important documents to the thumb drive.

Pillows

Did you know that it is recommended that you change (discard!) your pillows every couple of years? I did not know this but I was sure I had some pillows in my house that were easily 15 years old … and still being used on a daily basis. I quickly threw those away and replaced them with new ones. I was also quick to write down the month and year in permanent marker on the pillow tag to keep track of how new that particular pillow was. I only wish I had started marking all my pillows with dates immediately. I am sad to say that there are still a few pillows I am not sure if I need to replace them or not.

Prayer List

If praying is something you do or want to get better at, give yourself a little aid. If you have a computer, create a spreadsheet else just hand write it. The titles for each column could be: status, start date, prayer request, answer, end date. As you enter a new prayer, the status is "Open" and when it has been answered, the status changes to "Closed." Sort your list by descending order of status. Print the list and keep it near where you pray. You can hand write in new requests, but then update it once a week on the computer. If you don't have a computer, highlight the prayers that have been answered. You can continue to pray for the unanswered, un-highlighted prayers.

Purchases

When it comes time to buy "the right item," take a moment and look through magazines and catalogs to find the right item. If you are shopping for furniture, say a couch, thumb through as many house decorating magazines you can come by and rip out the pages where you like what you see. Keep the pages (store in a slash folder or file) and as time goes on, look at them again and make sure you still like them. Then, share the picture with your spouse or anyone else involved in the decision, and even the sales person at the store. This will help communications so you will be happy with what you purchase. This idea works well for furniture, clothes, gardening ideas, gadgets … what ever they have magazines and catalogs for, this idea works! This even works for Christmas shopping for other people. If you see an idea that you think that person would like, save the page. You might be surprised how many ideas you can collect.

The same idea works when you are researching the purchase of a product. Keep all the investigative information that you find in a folder. I know when we were shopping for a dishwasher, I knew what brand I wanted and I started to clip newspaper ads on the prices from the different stores. I could gather the clippings and compare them so I can readily determine who had the best price.

Purses

I don't know about you, but if you're like me, I'll store everything in my purse, even the kitchen sink. I'd start wondering why my purse was so heavy and why was I lugging this "suitcase" around? Then I decided to "go light.' I now have two purses, one large purse, that stays in the car and one light purse that I carry. The large purse contains the things I'd like to have with me, but they aren't urgent (like the kitchen sink). Do HIDE the large purse in the car. If you leave anything of importance in there, make sure you've written down the information on an index card (paper). I do leave a membership card in my large purse, and my library card etc. I have those numbers written on the separate index card and placed on my bulletin board. The light purse carries just my necessities—one lipstick, money, a few credit cards, cell phone, little spiral notebook, daily planner. Since I drive the same car around, I usually can grab what I need from the large purse most any time. And a nice benefit, you can have more fun picking out purses!

School Yearbook

If you *want* each of your children to own their own school yearbook, then this tidbit is not for you. But if you don't want to spend around $15.00 for a yearbook for each child then what do you do? Do you buy one and have them share it? Well, in some school environments, it's not that simple due to the fun tradition of "Yearbook Signing" where you go around and have everyone autograph and write comments or memories or phone numbers. My children weren't really interested in getting a yearbook but I didn't want them to miss out on the "Yearbook Signing" part. If I had thought of this dilemma sooner, I might have found an Autograph Book in a store. But, I didn't, and I couldn't, so I ended up buying a Journal Book for each child. A Journal Book is just a bound book with empty pages. I suggested they decorate the first page of the journal with the name of the school and the second page for the current school grade. Then they can pass the book around and ask friends to sign it in *that* grade section. They came back with several signed pages. The kids will keep their books until next year. They'll decorate the next blank page with the new grade, and have their friends sign after that, etc. Now they have one book for their entire school career with all of their friends' autographs. Make sure you buy a durable book.

Sewing Box

I had the hardest time finding a practical sewing box for the casual sewer. The sewing boxes I saw were more like a pretty basket with maybe one or two compartments. Not good enough! I have many different things that make up my sewing basket and I hardly sew! What I found, is that a TACKLE box is the perfect sewing kit! Try to find a sturdy one so you can leave the top open and it doesn't fall over. The tackle box is filled with dividers for thread, needles, pins, cushions etc.

Small Paper Bags (Lunch Size)

Fortunately, you can buy a hundred brown paper bags for pretty cheap. And, although you won't need all 100 for this idea, grab a couple. Place the "lunch" bags in inconspicuous places in the house to help you organize things. For instance, I keep two brown paper bags in my kitchen. One is for my "Campbell Soup" labels for school donation, and the other one is for "box tops for education" box tops (again, for school donations). I also use one to recycle cassette tapes that get donated to our church.

Soap—Those Little Left Over Pieces

If you have little kids who take baths, there is a use for those little pieces of soap that are left over from a normal bar of soap. Give them to the kids to play with in the bath. I used to get upset that the kids would take a brand new bar of soap and use it in the bath. The soap was left in the water for the duration of the bath and would easily be "wasted." Once I started to use the little left over pieces, we both "won." They could use the soap as long as the wanted (without me getting upset) and they were getting clean.

Socks?

I bet you didn't think there were organizational issues with socks? Well, here are a few ideas that may surprise you. First, "sort" them as you fold your laundry—avoid the temptation of putting them in a pile in the drawers. By rolling the socks into balls, you and your kids will have what they need when they need it instead of yelling "where's my other sock?!!" Sometimes we all overlook the obvious! You'll also notice you will have less number of unmatched socks.

Second, for those times that you do have unmatched sock, place them in one location (a drawer in the bedroom for example). Place everybody's unmatched socks there. Soon you'll find the partner to the spare without looking very hard ... it will be in that place sooner or later. And, if your kids ever make puppets out of socks, you can choose one from the unmatched pile. Usually I buy a package of socks so there are 6 similar socks. Sometimes my kids wear holes in one of the socks. I throw the other one in the unmatched draw. By the time they have worn out a hole in another matching sock, I now have a "new" pair of socks they can wear.

Another version to this is to buy socks that look different if your husband would like his own unique socks, not to be shared with the growing boys in the family. For instance, my husband's socks have gray on the heels and toes where my boys' socks are all white.

Sorting Clothes

If you have kids that are pretty close in size and sometimes, when you're folding their clothes, you cannot remember whose is whose then here's a great trick! On the label of the clothing item, use a permanent marker and make one "dot" on the label for all items belonging to the "largest/ oldest" child. Then, for the next child in line, add another "dot," etc. So the oldest wears the one dot clothes, the second wears the two dot clothes, the third …

Spare Keys

Are you in charge of spare keys for friends or family members or even for your own house? I was and now I am lost as to what keys belong to whom. I thought I'd remember by putting the keys on a "representative" key chain. For instance, if my brother was into a football team or college team, I'd find a key chain of that and place his keys on it. That works for some keys, but not all. A new solution I have found is to take a permanent marker and write the initials of the person who the keys belong to as soon as they give them to you. It's so simple and so easy. Now I know what keys belong to whom!

Supplies on Hand

This section lists a few typical items that are good to have around the house. If you "stock-up" on these items, you will have them handy when you really need them. This way you can shop when things are on sale or when you are out anyway and have time for these purchases.

- Gift paper — baby, pastels, kids birthdays, adult birthdays, general
- Greeting cards — Birthday — Humorous, Birthday — Friendship, Birthday — Family Related, Belated Birthdays, Anniversary, Thank You notes
- Wine — a great gift to bring over to friends for a casual occasion
- Knickknack gifts — stationary, picture frames, vases, decorative pens, and memo pads
- Garage sale items—extra plates and plant holders. The plate can be used to bring baked goods to a friend and then leave the plate—you don't have to think about getting it returned to you. Plus, a friend can always use a new entertainment plate. Or, stock up on plant pots. When you need a gift, go to the local store and buy a plant but save money by using a pot you've already picked up at a garage sale (the prices of ceramic planters is surprisingly high!).
- Markers—a great time to buy markers is in August, even if you don't have school age kids. The cost of a package of markers is reduced dramatically this time of year. Save, save, save!

Toddlers Sleeping Habits

What does this title mean? Well, my 3-year-old kept waking in the middle of the night throughout the year. He did not know how to tell time yet (even on a digital clock) so I had to figure out a way to let him know it was NOT yet time to wake up. Place a timer on a night light in the child's room and set the timer for your child's sleep time. Instruct the child that, should they awaken and the light is ON, they must stay in bed and go back to sleep. When the light is OFF, it is OK to get out of bed. This may even work with a 2-year-old (it has with mine!).

Vacations

To enhance your memories of your vacation, bring a special piece of paper with you while on vacation. Label the paper with each day of your vacation (both MM/DD/YYYY and name of day). As you go through your vacation, write down the events each day. When vacation is over, you can store this with your pictures or scrapbook. Vacations are such a cherished time for the families, this piece of paper will remind everyone of the special events. I have started to include this paper in the family photo album, as well.

Warranties

Sometimes I buy a product because of its warranty. Sometime a product that I have will break and I wonder what the warranty is on it. If you have a good filing system, as recommended in Chapter 1, "File Drawer," you can find your warranty for the product with ease. However, finding the receipt for the warranty to show it is active is another story.

Now, as soon as I purchase the product, I staple the receipt or a copy of the receipt to the warranty and then file it away. This is a much more productive process!

Wines—the Ones That I Like

If you drink wine and are searching for the ones that you really enjoy, you may find this trick helpful. I try all different labeled wines and I purchase them from different stores. I got very discourage when I found a wine I really liked but I couldn't remember where I purchased it from. So I started to mark the wine label with a code or initial of the store that I bought it from. It just made life so much easier to go back to that particular store and look for the wine I enjoy.

To take that one step further, I started to list wines either on an index card or in the "Little Spiral Notebook" from Chapter 1 in three categories: Good, OK, and Bad. In each column, I'd list the name of the wine, year, and store "code." As I am choosing new wines, I can look at this list and see if I had bought it before or if I want a "known quantity," I search out the wine that I know we like (in the Good or OK column). And the important part to all of this is to keep your list in your purse or somewhere "handy" for the next time you go wine shopping. You will be knowledgeable about what you like and not "wasting" your money on something you may have already tried and decided you didn't like! (I did that once and got mad at myself for not being smarter!).

Wrapping Paper, Storage

A great way to store wrapping paper is in empty wine boxes. You can get them from a liquor store. These boxes are sturdy boxes, with dividers in them thus creating "sections" (usually 12 sections). The dividers allow you to store the wrapping paper in an upright position. This way, it is easy to see and it shouldn't get ripped. You can even store the extra cuttings in the sections as well. Just curl up the extra wrapping (as if it were on an imaginary tube) and place in a free section.

Appendix A
Grocery Categories

Air Freshener
Aluminum Foil
Apple Sauce
Baby - Diapers
Baby - Food
Baby Wipes
Bacon
Baking Staples
Batteries
BBQ Sauce
Biscuits
Bread Crumbs
Butter
Cakes
Candy
Cat Food
Cat Litter
Cereal
Cheese
Cleaning - Misc.
Cleaning - All Purpose
Cleaning - Bathroom
Cleaning - Carpet
Cleaning - Dishes
Cleaning - Drain
Cleaning - Floor
Cleaning - Floor Wax
Cleaning - Furniture
Cleaning - Toilet
Cleaning - Windows
Cocoa
Coffee
Coffee - Instant
Cold Cuts
Cookies
Crackers (Chips)
Dog Food
Film
Frozen
Frozen - Vegetables
Garbage Bags
Gum
Hair
Hot Dogs
Ice Cream
Ice Tea
Jelly
Juices
Ketchup
Kleenex
Light Bulbs
Mayonnaise
Medicine
Medicine - Aspirin
Medicine - Children's
Medicine - Colds

Appendix A
Grocery Categories cont.

Medicine - Lozenges
Mustard
Nuts
Oil
Pancakes (plus Syrup)
Pasta
Peanut Butter
Personal
Personal - Lotions
Personal - Mouthwash
Personal - Toothpaste
Pickles
Pizza
Pop
Rice
Salad Dressings
Salsa
Soap
Soup
Sour Cream
Spices
Spray Starch
Tacos
Tea
Toilette Paper
Tomato (sauce/paste etc.)
Tuna
Washing Detergents
Yeast
Yogurt

Appendix B
Sample Packing List

	Dad	Mom	Kid1	Kid2	Kid3	Food	
A Coats							
A Snow gear							
A Shirts, sleeveless							
A Hats							Cereal
A PJ's							Pancake Mix
A Shoes							Syrup
A Shirts, short sleeved							Carrots
A Shirts, long sleeved							Raisins
A Shorts							Paper towels
A Long pants							Napkins
A Sweat shirt							Canned vegetables
A Slippers							Bread
A Socks							Peanut butter
A Sunglasses							Jelly
A Swim suits							Spaghetti O's
A Toothbrush							Cheese
A Underwear							Sloppy Joe, canned
A Vitamins							Hamb. buns, 2 pkgs
A Water shoes							Oranges
K Bibs							Yogurt
K Blankets							Hot dogs
K Bubbles							Hot dog buns
K Diaper bag							Ketchup
K Diapers							Spaghetti sauce
K Wipes							Coffee
H Beach towels							Pop
H Address book							Napkins

Appendix B
Sample Packing List, cont.

	Dad	Mom	Kid1	Kid2	Kid3	Food	
H Atlas/Map							Cooking spray
H Back Pack							Saran wrap
H Bible Study							Canned juices
H Cameras etc							Breakfast bars
H Cell phone/charger							Pretzels
H Food for traveling							Crackers
H Laundry detergent							Orange Juice
H Money							Milk
H Pens/Pencils							Butter
Rafts/pool stuff							3 lb hamburger
H Sunscreen							Chicken nuggets
H Hotel/airline info							Ham, lunch meat
H Waist Bag							Apples
H Water bottle							Apple slicer
K Bath Toys							Grapes
K Books							Mac n cheese
K Craft box							Beer
K Eating supplies							Wine
(cups, plates)							
K Juice box holder							Chocolate milk mix
K Little Cars							Freeze pops
K Medicine							Popcorn
K Puzzles							Salsa/chips
K Sand toys							Spaghetti
K Strollers							
K Stuffed Animals							
K Surprise Toys							

Appendix B
Sample Packing List, cont.

	Dad	Mom	Kid1	Kid2	Kid3	Food	
K Toys							
K Train + Tracks							
K Videos / DVDs							
D Doppler Bag							
M Bath. suit cover up							
M Cosmetics/bag							
H Spare Car Key							
M/D Day timer							
M/D Deodorant							
H Walkie Talkie							
M Jewelry							
M Makeup							
M Nail polish etc.							
A Reading Material							
M Slips/nylons							
M/D Wallet							
H Boom box/ipod							

Legend

A	All
K	Kids
M	Mom
D	Dad
H	Home

Printed in the United States
202177BV00003B/388-396/P

9 781596 635722